Quilts from Happy Hands™

19 Original Quilts • Complete Patterns & Instructions
Quiltmaking Techniques Section by Colette Wolff

Sandra Lee Wright

Happy Hands™ Publishing Company
Fort Worth, Texas

Sandra Lee Wright, Editor of *Quilts from Happy Hands*, has enjoyed a long and productive career in the field of needlework and craft publishing.

Her background includes writing and producing a large series of instruction books dealing with a wide variety of subjects for the handicrafts division of Tandy Corporation. She has also served as Editorial Assistant for both the *Craftsman* and *Decorating & Craft Ideas* magazines. In 1976, while at *Decorating & Craft Ideas*, Sandra researched and authored the popular year-long series, "Crafts of America: 1776-1976" which described 18th century handcrafts and provided projects for their modern counterparts.

An avid needleworker and creative sewing enthusiast herself, Sandra continues to broaden her knowledge of various types of needlework through constant study. She is presently Editor of *Needlecraft for Today* magazine and Senior Editor of Happy Hands Library.

ISBN: 0-941468-01-1
Library of Congress Catalog Card Number: 81-48007
Printed in the United States of America
Copyright © 1981 by Happy Hands Publishing Company
4949 Byers, Ft. Worth, Texas 76107

Happy Hands Library

President and Publisher: Steven A. Bassion
Vice-President and Editorial Director: Fredrica Daugherty
Senior Editor: Sandra Lee Wright
Technical Editor: Colette Wolff
Art Director: Patricia Catherine Williams

Quilts from Happy Hands

Photography:
    Scott Lennox, pp. front cover, 7, 8, 9, 10, 11,
    14, 26-27, 30-31, 34-35, 39, 40-41, 42-43, 44-45, 46-47,
    52-53, 54-55, 56-57.
    Larry Dockery: pp. back cover, 15, 17, 18-19, 22-23, 25,
    28-29.
    Michael Cagen: pp. 8, 13.
    Robert E. Coyle: pp. 9, 21.
    David Sweitzer, pp. 9, 37.
    Julius Kubin: pp. 9, 51.

Photographic Assistance: Donna Buie; Randee Paur.
Techniques illustrations: Colette Wolff.
Quilt and instructions illustrations: Fain **Hancock.**
Pattern illustrations: Patty Cox; Jack **Cox.**
Art Production: Fain Hancock; Patty Cox.
Editorial Assistants: Doug Nichols; Cindy Lea Arbelbide; Margaret Dittman.

Grateful acknowledgment is made by the author to the four women whose quilts are represented in this book: Colette Wolff, Mary Borkowski, Diann Logan and Kathy Sue Guillow; to Donna Rabe who pieced and quilted the Flowering Plum quilt; to Nina Hall who pieced Starry Night and Susi Stewart who quilted it.

Printed by R. R. Donnelley & Sons Company
Separation by Wilson Engraving Co., Inc.
Typesetting by Crosby Typesetting Co., Inc.

Contents

Introduction 7

Designers & Their Quilts

Colette Wolff 13
Starry Night 14
Queen's Petticoat 16
Flowering Plum 18

Mary Borkowski 21
Hawaiian Fruit Trees 22
Stars Over Hawaii 24
Christmas Star 26
Sunstar 28
Along the River 30
Country Rose 32
Jackie's Tulips 34

Diann Logan 37
Joanne's Quilt 38
Vanishing Point 40
Evolution 42
Sweet Dreams 44
Holy Man 46
Symphony in F 48

Kathy Sue Guillow 51
Oriental Blossom 52
Peach Blossom 54
American Indian 56

Techniques 59

Help for Color Shy Quilters 59
Sensibly Speaking 65
The Size Question 65
Decisions in the Fabric Store 66
The Nuts and Bolts 67
That Enlarging Chore 68
Templates 68
Cutting 70
Piecing the Blocks 73
Applique 80
Assembling the Top 84
Quilting: The Design 85
Quilting: The Process 88
Binding the Edge 93
The Signature 97
Display and Care 97

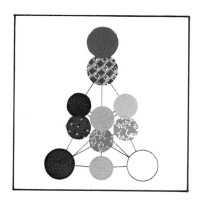

Instructions & Patterns

Starry Night 99
Queen's Petticoat 105
Flowering Plum 111
Hawaiian Fruit Trees....................121
Stars Over Hawaii 124
Christmas Star..........................127
Sunstar 133
Along the River 138
Country Rose 145
Jackie's Tulips 148
Joanne's Quilt 154
Vanishing Point 156
Evolution 159
Sweet Dreams 163
Holy Man..............................166
Symphony in F 170

Oriental Blossom 173
Peach Blossom 180
American Indian 185

Resources..........................190

Index.............................191

Introduction

"Happy hands make happy hearts" . . . from this verse Happy Hands Publishing Company took its name and in 1978 began publishing a how-to magazine for women interested in needlearts, *Needlecraft for Today*. All the needlearts were represented: knit, crochet, needlepoint, embroidery of all kinds, lacemaking — and the consistent favorite among readers, quiltmaking. In every issue a quilt was presented, and every quilt was fresh and original. We soon realized that one of the greatest areas of expression for the needlearts was in this medium.

The response to the magazine was overwhelming and immediate . . . readers appreciated the quality projects offered and the fact that patterns and instructions for every project shown were in the magazine. The most important aspect of the magazine's success was in its free-lance designers. They made the magazine work because they created projects that readers wanted.

Two and a half years after the start of *Needlecraft for Today*, Happy Hands Publishing Company began a new magazine called *Needle & Thread*. Its goal was to provide original creative sewing projects of all kinds from garment making to toys . . . anything to do with hand and machine sewing. Again, the response was immediate, and again the quality quilt projects that the designers gave contributed to the magazine's broad appeal.

Many beautiful quilts have appeared on the pages of *Needlecraft for Today* and *Needle & Thread*, and from those we have selected nineteen designed by four talented designers: Colette Wolff, Mary Borkowski, Diann Logan and Kathy Sue Guillow. We want to do more than give you a book of lovely quilts. We want to introduce you to these women and perhaps give you an insight into how they came to create these quilts and what each one means to them. Inspiration is their motivation, and quilts provide a warm and wonderful vehicle for its expression.

Considering the amount of time involved, quiltmaking has to be a labor of love. The woman who makes a quilt puts much of herself into it . . . in its design, color and style. When you find a quilt you are attracted to, don't you begin wondering about the woman who made it . . . what she was like, where she lived, was she young or not so young? Keeping in mind that each tiny piece of fabric probably represented some part of her life, it's fun to look at the patterns and prints and think, "I'll bet this fabric was left from her little girl's first school dress, or that white on black feather print was probably from the dress she wore to church; the tiny stripe could have been left over from her husband's dress shirt."

Once while buying a lovely old wool pieced quilt from an elderly couple, I spread the quilt out on the floor of their living room to see the entire pattern. The man, in his eighties I'm sure, said, "Look ma, that black is from the suit I wore to our wedding, and that gray pin stripe was the jacket I wore in our act" (they had been in vaudeville). That quilt means so much more to me now. I would have loved it anyway, but now I feel I'm taking care of it for them so it's very precious

"We want to do more than give you a book of lovely quilts . . . we want to introduce you to these women."

> "...there is no stereotyped quilter; the common ground is a love of quiltmaking."

Colette Wolff

to me. It makes me wish I could meet the woman and her family who made every quilt I love . . . and treasure . . . and wonder about.

We want you to meet the four women who designed the quilts shown in this book, to get to know something about them, their families and especially what each quilt meant to them as it was created. As the material was assembled a sort of reverse coincidence was discovered. The four women whose quilts were to be included were very different from each other. Not just different personalities, but geographically, stage of life — everything about them was different. This realization helps prove that there is no stereotyped quilter; the common ground is a love of quiltmaking. Colette Wolff is a cosmopolitan woman with a professional background in acting. She lives in New York City, is married with no children. Diann Logan is a young mother and rock and roll musician living in Denver, Colorado; Mary Borkowski is a widow who lives in Dayton, Ohio and has enjoyed a high level of recognition for her quilts by museums and quilt collectors of note; Kathy Sue Guillow is relatively new to quilt-

Diann Logan

Mary Borkowski

Kathy Sue Guillow

making. She is the mother of grown children and lives in Whittier, California.

There are men quilters . . . some have received much acclaim for their quilt designs and rightfully so. However, except for a very few brave males, quilting is a feminine pursuit. It, more than any other medium, has offered women artistic expression regardless of their circumstances. If you ever have the opportunity, see the film, "Quilts in Women's Lives." This award-winning 28 minute film (see Resources) captures the essence of what quilts can mean to women through a series of portraits of traditional quiltmakers and provides an insight into the spirit of these women who are the basis for this continuing tradition of quiltmaking. Seven women, among them a Californian Mennonite, a black Mississippian and a Bulgarian immigrant, talk about their art and the influences on it. To quote the New York Film Festival, "Quilts in Women's Lives' dispels any notion that 'little old ladies' make quilts because they have nothing better to do."

Quilting can be a solitary pursuit. More often it provides women with an opportunity to share,

> **"Smaller groups of women ally themselves for the pure pleasure of quilting in the company of other quilters."**

encourage each other . . . or just be together working on a project. Quilting bees are still happening all over the country, usually as a church-related activity to be used as fund-raisers. Other social clubs sometimes decide to make a group-project quilt to raffle as a means of sponsoring an activity. Smaller groups of women ally themselves for the pure pleasure of quilting in the company of other quilters. Classes are another way women get together to quilt. The teacher shares her knowledge with other women who

want to learn to make better quilts and with women who have never quilted in their lives, but want to learn.

Once hooked, quilting can become something of an obsession (or, call it avocation). There are huge quilt conferences held all over the United States which offer advanced workshops in various phases of quiltmaking, lectures on specific areas of the quilt world combined with luncheons and banquets where all the participants join each other for a meal and a lecture.

Quiltmaking provides a bonding for women of all ages and lifestyles. The involvement with quilts provides them with a shared interest from which lifelong friendships can develop.

We know you'll enjoy these nineteen original designs, and that you'll probably want to make one or more of them for your home. We also believe the quilts will mean more to you because you'll know the stories behind them, and these stories will unfold as you add the fabric of your own life.

"... these stories will unfold as you add the fabric of your own life."

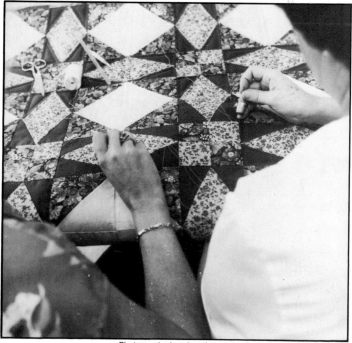

Photographed on location at the Quilt Box, Ft. Worth, Texas.

Designer:

Colette Wolff

Quilt designers share an interesting quality . . . they "see" things differently. It is a quality they have in common with artists as a whole — they interpret life through a special sense that allows them to transfer what they see into an art form. When Colette Wolff describes the inspiration for Starry Night as being a memory of seeing the aurora borealis, she is verbalizing that quality.

Colette began sewing squares of fabric together as a child, inspired by a grandmother who used to make tied quilts on the dining room table. She and her husband now live in the middle of Manhattan, two blocks from Central Park, a short walk or subway ride from New York's major museums and performance and shopping centers — not an area particularly noted for its quiltmaking activities.

Her teaching experience began when she accepted a position teaching crafts at the women's house of detention, a prison facility in New York City. As Colette relates, " . . . an experience which presented challenges not usually associated with the genteel teaching of crafts." She began teaching quiltmaking ten years ago at a craft gallery shop in New York called Performer's Outlet; went on to teach quiltmaking, soft toymaking, dollmaking, stitchery, color and design for the Elder Craftsmen Special Project, an unusual craft education agency that instructs teachers, either staff or volunteer, who work in New York City's senior citizen facilities. Colette also taught quiltmaking and dollmaking workshops for Museums Collaborative: the Museum of Contemporary Crafts' Outreach Program.

The business of crafts has many levels and Colette has worked in virtually all of them: she was involved in the operation of two craft shops, has been a production craftsman, has written articles for craft magazines, and has exhibited in national shows. Now she is a designer, writer and illustrator in the textile craft field for her own business, and travels from time to time giving special workshops on three-dimensional fabric design, color and design, quiltmaking and other craft related subjects.

A change in her priorities came in 1980 when she resigned all teaching positions to devote herself full-time to the operation and growth of Platypus, a business that produces and sells patterns and cloth kits for crafts and clothes. Platypus began in 1970 with mimeographed doll and toy patterns, continued through a series of mail-order catalogs offering an ever-expanding inventory of professionally-printed patterns and is now moving into the production of quality kits for dolls and quilted items.

As Colette so aptly sums up her career, "I find it constantly amazing, particularly after years of specialized theatrical training at the University of Wisconsin and in professional classes in New York City, and after an early career as an actress working for television and industrials, in summer stock and off-Broadway, to be doing professionally what started so easily and pleasurably as a childhood activity."

Starry Night

Sometimes on clear winter nights in Wisconsin, where I grew up, the horizon would show faint shimmers of the northern lights or aurora borealis, blending into a skyful of stars above. I remember my father explaining to me what those rays of colors were; I remember how large and brilliant the stars seemed to be in the clear, sharp air; and I remember shivering because it was so cold and so impressive. Somehow that early memory, and a pattern for a quilt block, came together in my head. In a manner as mysterious as the northern lights themselves, the quilt was all there before I ever put a line on paper.

I like off-center designs that can be set in many ways. I like the thought that others can use the Starry Night pattern, arrange the blocks to interact in a different way, and add their own creative vision to what I began.

—COLETTE WOLFF

Queen's Petticoat

I wanted to do something with the nine-patch. I wanted to see if I could create a design that someone else hadn't already invented and added to that large classification of quilt patterns. I wanted the design to be composed of squares and triangles only so that it would be easy enough for beginners to use as a first quilt, just as so many women in the past used a nine-patch in one of its many design ramifications for their first quilt.

The design evolved through many trials on paper before it arrived at the final version. When I finished making the quilt, I brought it to a quiltmaking class I was teaching. At that time I didn't have a name for the pattern. I asked the class for suggestions. Frances Fixler, with hardly a pause to consider, said, "I think it should be called the Queen's Petticoat." And so it is.

Because it is an asymmetrical design, the blocks set into any number of different arrangements and effects. Perhaps other quiltmakers will discover these and give their quilts companion names — the King's Mantle, the Duke's Doublet, the Duchess's Jewels — a royal houseful of quilts from humble nine-patch beginnings.

—COLETTE WOLFF

16

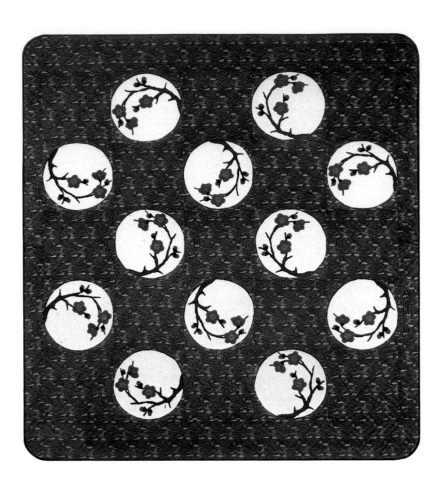

Flowering Plum

There weren't any other quilts with oriental themes in January of 1979, at least none that I was aware of. I don't recall what started me thinking about an oriental-inspired quilt at that time, but suddenly the idea was there. I went to the Metropolitan Museum and wandered through the Oriental Galleries. I looked through art books with reproductions of lovely Japanese scrolls. The flowering plum motif appeared again and again — it symbolizes longevity and the continuation of life — and gradually it emerged as the theme, the design I wanted to interpret in fabric. The quilting motifs are interpretations of textile patterns.

I wanted the colors of the quilt to reflect a shadowy interior with circular windows that show a plum branch flowering in the brightness outside. I searched in numerous fabric stores for a particular tone of gray-green cotton and, finally, I found one bolt of expensive, silky, Italian cotton with a color and pattern that captured the appropriate mood. I sent all the materials, patterns, directions, and a sample block to Donna Rabe in Idaho Falls, Idaho who labored many months to complete the finished quilt with its extensive and intricate quilting.

—COLETTE WOLFF

Designer:
Mary Borkowski

Impressions from nature, bold colors and graphic design are the elements that produce the visual impact of Mary Borkowski's quilts. Her work combines art with impeccable craftsmanship — a combination found in the work of all four women represented within these pages. Good design is extremely important, but it is wasted if the execution is anything short of excellent.

Among Mary's publishing credits (in addition to Happy Hands Publishing Company) are magazines such as *McCall's Needlework & Crafts, Quilter's Newsletter, Nimble Needle Treasures* and *Embroiderer's Journal*. Her quilts have appeared in numerous books: *Twentieth Century Folk Art & Artists, Quilts in America, Anyone Can Quilt, Portrait of America, Art of Embroidery* and many more.

Her quilts hang in the most prestigious museums in the United States including the Smithsonian, the Museum of American Folk Art and the LBJ Library and Museum. She has shown her needlework in fairs, art institutes, universities and galleries all over the country.

Let's listen as Mary tells the background story of her life.

"As long as I can remember quilts and quilting have been a part of my life. My mother and grandmother were fine seamstresses, making many quilts and fancy clothes. In those days of ruffles, laces and ribbons, one had to be good with a needle to produce nice things.

"My mother always had a quilt or other needlework project going to pick up in an idle moment, but with five children, 32 dogs (my father had kennels) and eighteen boarders each summer, she never seemed to quite finish anything. Being very frugal, she would buy limited yardage, instead of over-buying as I do. To me, it is much better to have too much fabric than too little, because often enough, if you run out of fabric the store will be sold out and your quilt is ruined. I always call for a generous amount of fabric when describing how to make one of my quilts just to make sure there is plenty.

"I was born and raised at a summer resort called Sulphur Lick Springs near Chillicothe, Ohio. Droves of people came by train to the resort and were carried up the hill to the hotel via surrey and horses. My mother had a houseful of guests each summer . . . her homecooking was much appreciated by the vacationers.

"The Great Depression struck early at Sulphur Lick Springs with almost no guests arriving as the economy began to collapse. One late summer Sunday afternoon, a Dayton man and his family were driving through sightseeing when their car ran off the rainslick dirt road and slipped down into a ravine and stopped in a precarious spot thanks to some trees. My father and brother rescued the entire family plus their dog and car by pulling them out with chains. The grateful man was manager of a washing machine company in Dayton, and he offered my father a job in recompense for saving his family. My father immediately accepted his offer . . . we abandoned our large house, put everything in a big truck just like in the movie "Grapes of Wrath" and took off.

"In two months the factory closed its doors and that left us with practically nothing. My oldest brother got a job in a garage, my younger brother a paper route, my sister in a tea room, my mother sewed for people and we got by. But that is another story.

"My mother picked up her quilting from time to time, and when I was fourteen I selected a Laura Wheeler pattern, the Fan, from the newspaper and made my first quilt.

"Years passed and in 1948 while recovering from a long illness at my mother's home in Washington C. H., Ohio I made my first grand prize winning quilt — the Poinsettia. My next quilt was Roses and Leaves and it was also a grand prize winner. I never again made a quilt from another person's pattern, with one exception. Jackie Fowler wanted an exact duplicate of a Hawaiian quilt pictured in Robert Bishop's book, *New Discoveries in American Quilts* and I made it for her."

Hawaiian Fruit Trees

My sister brought back a shopping bag decorated with palm trees from a trip she made to Hawaii. I made this quilt based on her recollections of that trip as a memory quilt in her honor.

The six basic colors from which all colors emerge have always fascinated me and I have used them over and over in different forms in many quilts. In this quilt I made them in a balanced pattern of fruit. The red striped borders I adapted from the frames I designed in a bicentennial quilt. The green and red borders were meant to compliment the twelve framed trees.

—MARY BORKOWSKI

Stars Over Hawaii

This is the second quilt in honor of my sister, Dorothy Heery. Her last vacation to Hawaii provided her with much pleasure and she returned with many wonderful stories of the islands — her excursion down into a volcano, trips to the little shops and the wonderful, delicious food.

The Hawaiian name for this quilt is "Nohoku Iluna I Hawaii" and it was inspired in part by the "Comb of Kaiulaiani" which hangs in the Honolulu Academy of Arts in Hawaii. The green over yellow appliques have many stars and different sizes of fish. The center parts resemble the delicious sweet-smelling pineapples. In the center is the yellow sun-star, the source of all life.

—MARY BORKOWSKI

Christmas Star

A postcard in a magazine gave me the idea for this quilt. I wanted to make a star similar to one you would use on top of a Christmas tree. The small sections are merely parts of the whole and the red lines of quilting in backstitch alternating with white quilting lines are meant to convey the reflections such as those found in a diamond. All the other aspects of the design from the center silver star to the quilting designs are based on the religious part of Christmas.

During my grade school years, my brothers and sister and I accompanied my father to the woods at Christmas time seeking just the right tree for chopping. Back home we made stars from cardboard covered in tin foil which we joyously hung on the tree along with strung cranberries and popcorn.

—MARY BORKOWSKI

Sunstar

The original large star which appears in this quilt was first made for a neighbor of mine who verbally described a star motif she had seen and wanted for a quilt. From her description I designed the star, but she ended up not using it after all. So I made a quilt with the pattern using it as the focal point on all the blocks.

Using the red and blue sun/sky colors, which with yellow are the three primary colors, a quilt was created. The bright yellow is the glow that covers the earth from the sun as it passes over, giving the tranquility in the blue of the sky. The quilting lines just seemed to fall in place as I proceeded. In this quilt they were not planned ahead of time.

—MARY BORKOWSKI

28

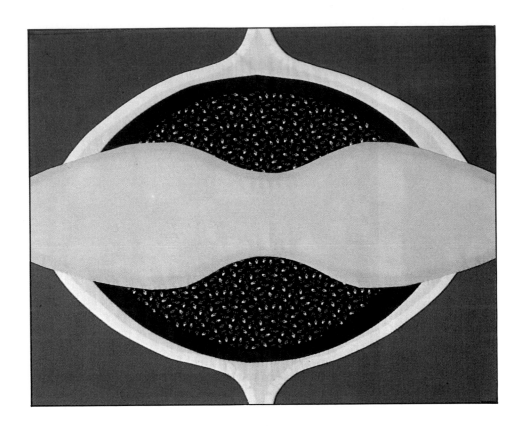

Along the River

This quilt design goes back to childhood memories at Sulphur Lick Springs, Ohio. Almost every day my brothers, sister and I would walk the two miles down into the "holler" and out across the railroad tracks down a path through high weeds and grass to the swimming hole of the creek. I can still see that running water rippling along, sometimes swiftly, sometimes still, but always moving and splashing onto the flowered grassy banks, beckoning us for an afternoon of fun. Such is a carefree childhood from which come ideas later in life. They seem so sweet looking back on them.

—MARY BORKOWSKI

Country Rose

I have never forgotten the real country rose, the one with five open flat petals with yellow centers, that used to grow wild in the countryside. They were abundant on the site of my grandmother's maiden home which long ago burned down. I was born near there, and along with other children explored all the fields, woods and valleys. Wild flowers were everywhere and we so loved to pick the roses, violets and tulips.

The quilting on this quilt is meant to convey the impression of the old wooden country fences prevalent in that part of Ohio. Most of them included a stile which was a group of steps that went to the top of the fence and then down the other side. Wonderful memories!

—MARY BORKOWSKI

Jackie's Tulips

This quilt was inspired by another tulip quilt created especially for Jackie Fowler. It now has a permanent home in the Museum of American Folk Art in New York City.

This second quilt of Jackie's Tulips has basically the same colors but in an entirely new and different arrangement. The color scheme first selected is striking but the fleeting tulips done in color stitching create a subtle effect. Varying the original pattern offers the idea that anyone can take a given pattern and create their own in their own style and color scheme.

—MARY BORKOWSKI

Designer:

Diann Logan

After spending the years from 1967 to 1972 studying vocal music at the University of Denver and playing keyboard and singing for several Denver rock bands, Diann Logan was delighted to find that the geometry of her other love, patchwork, was very similar to the precision of classical music. Now she says when she can't write a song to fit an occasion, she makes a quilt instead.

Diann's quilts have been shown in over two dozen juried and judged shows and exhibits.

Diann relates how she began quilting and something of her life:

"I was born in Dallas, Texas and grew up in Kansas, Oklahoma, Montana and Wyoming, finally parking long enough to graduate from high school in Riverton, Wyoming. I began studying music early in life — piano at eight, followed by organ lessons at 12 and voice lessons at 16. I have been a performer most of my life and even did a stint as a church organist/choir director from seventh grade through graduation. After that I was on stage, if not for music, then in drama or speech classes or college operas.

"I was too busy to be a political activist in college . . . and had the luxury of closing my practice room door to the rest of the world. I came into feminism in the early '70s shortly after my daughter was born. I'm still not a marcher, but I do consider myself an activist, a humanist, a pacifist — trying to say something with my art that moves people. I never dreamed I'd be into visual art. My pictures in grade school always drew howls of laughter from my peers and sniffs from teachers. Therefore, I was turned off to the notion of drawing at a very early age, and art class was always a misery for me. In fact I still can't draw, have no art training and really don't know how I do what I do.

"In 1979 I felt my quilting technique had improved enough to withstand public scrutiny, so I began exhibiting my quilts. The future looks like more of the same — always trying to expand patchwork, while making the stitches smaller.

"Technically, I'm committed to machine-piecing and hand-quilting. None of my quilts are ever farmed-out. Every stitch is done by me. There is no such thing as an average quilt, but the simplest designs require at least four hours of labor per square foot. Designs with lots of quilting may take ten hours per square foot to complete. Probably half the craft of quilting is training the body to sit still while the mind and fingers fly.

"The influence of quilting could have only come from one source — my paternal grandmother, Eva Francis Coker Fincher. As a pre-schooler, I was at her house on more than one occasion when her church group came over to 'set 'n quilt a spell.' I was mildly interested in what they were doing, but much more fascinated by the feeling in my grandma's little living room. It was warm and alive in there. The afternoon would pass in a jumble of food, laughter and talk and quilting. I think it dawned on me, even then, that the quilting was just an excuse to be together and let out their feelings. 'They wuz all jes' ole widder-wimen, and they jes' got kinely lonesum, you know, not havin' no family any more.' Some were too infirm to get there without a cane or a daughter to drive them, but not the foulest weather could deter them. I remember particularly one afternoon in the midst of a nasty sleet and ice storm (the kind that southern Oklahoma is famous for), and there they were, a dozen or so of them with their 'I declare' accents and thimbles flying. Every so often they'd get up to stretch, walking around the edge of the frame to 'ooh' and 'aah' over the fine stitches that somebody else had laid on. It seemed to me that 'nary a cross word' passed over that frame. It seemed to me that they loved each other and they had a rip-snortin' good time. I'm sure the craving for that feeling had something to do with my current obsession with quilting."

Joanne's Quilt

Use your imagination, if you will, to picture two 13-year-old girls spending a week's vacation from school — in the hospital. In those days many local merchants displayed signs in the window which read, 'no dogs or Indians allowed.' Given the highly segregated community we lived in, it must have been a bureaucratic mistake that landed Joanne and I in the same room. After two days of silence, we discovered that by joining forces against the nurses we stood a better chance of getting extra snacks. Once the ice was broken we couldn't stop talking. By the end of the week we had both changed our views about racial hatred. I cherish the hand-beaded necklace she gave me— a gesture of hope that we could bridge the gap between us. This quilt is for Joanne, for harmony and understanding, for the day when all humans will have freedom, equality and love in their hearts.

—DIANN LOGAN

Vanishing Point

There is repetition here, always in the same order, each color
following the outline of the one preceding it. The "point" at
the bottom of the quilt is lost several times and then reappears,
only to be lost again. What is the "point" of existence?
Are we in danger of losing the point when we repeat the same
life patterns, always in the same order, each action following
the outline of the one preceding it?

—DIANN LOGAN

Evolution

Evolution is about growth and change. The green/brown color scheme is symbolic of the cycle of change as we see it repeated every spring. From the predominant brown earth of winter comes the lushness of spring growth. Spring is perhaps the most obvious example that while growth potential may be hidden from our view, while the barren apple tree branches of February show no promise, always underneath is the mystery of life.

—DIANN LOGAN

42

43

Sweet Dreams

Commonly wished to children as they go 'night-night', and sometimes wished between lovers or others with close ties. Since the dreaming mind takes the material for its stories from the storehouse of the waking mind, Sweet Dreams are unlikely if the waking mind is filled with stress or anxiety. A wish for Sweet Dreams is really a wish for a Sweet Life. Let the wish expand beyond just those who sleep under this quilt. What a Utopia we could have here if no one went to sleep hungry . . . or angry . . . or depressed . . . or . . .

—DIANN LOGAN

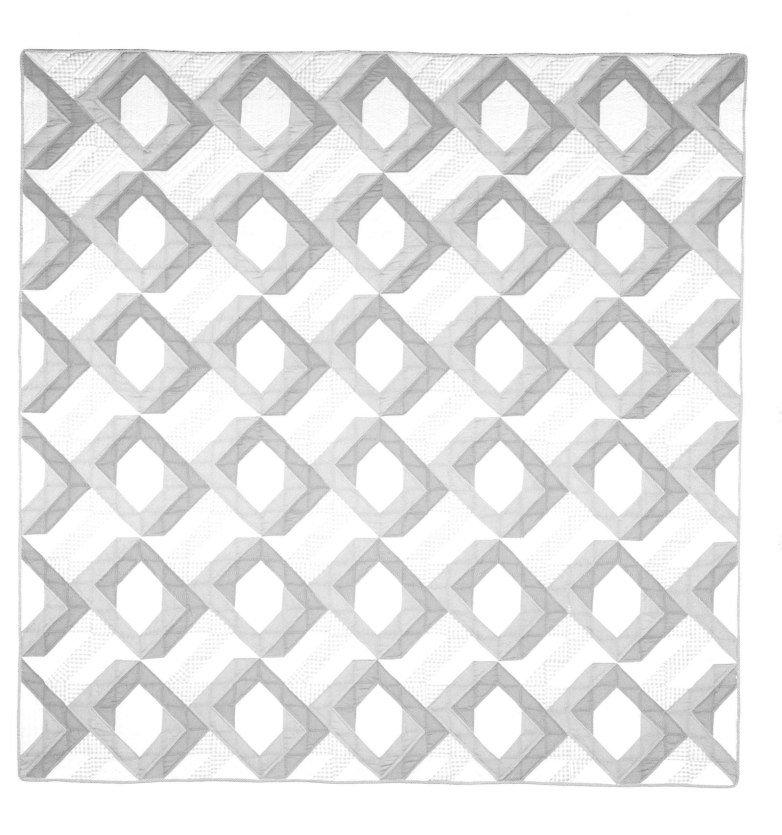

Holy Man

This quilt is made of variations on the Greek and Maltese crosses. The cross is an important symbol in all religions for many differing theologies. I view it as a sign of the wholeness of the Universe, encompassing all directions at once. Every religion marks out certain holy men as fitting examples of the heights which human spirituality can attain. This quilt is for one and all who seek to know. "For the one who is aware. For the one who has balance between light and dark, hot and cold, good and evil. For the one who accepts the total integration of the Universe. Such a one has no name, travels incognito, always surrounded by white love light."

—DIANN LOGAN

47

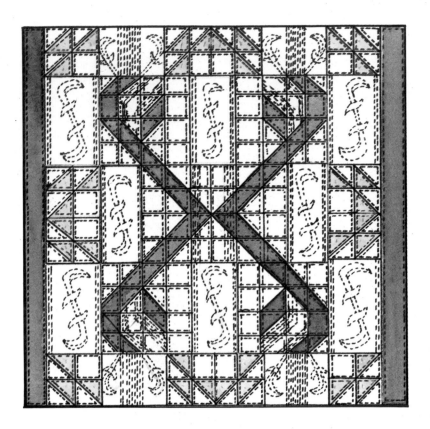

Symphony in F

The classical symphony is not randomly composed. Rather it is constructed around a framework — it has a blueprint or pattern which the composer follows. A symphony has a theme which is presented at the beginning of the piece. Thereafter the composer "plays" with that theme and fills in the spaces between its repetition. As it repeats, it may be inverted, restated, mirrored or embellished. It may return in a different key. It may entwine with itself or with a secondary symphonic style. I've never written a symphony, but this quilt was designed in symphonic style.

A theme — the blue F's — recurs in many different forms. The quilted F's could be thought of as a different "key", and the yellow triangles represent the secondary theme. At the conclusion of its perforamnce, this symphony stands as a union of all its smaller elements. The original theme is of importance, not as it stands on its own, but as an integral part of the whole.

—DIANN LOGAN

Techniques

by Colette Wolff

After looking at the pictures of the nineteen quilts in this book, there may be one quilt that you remember above all the others. You go back to look at it again. It fills your eyes with pleasurable sensations. You linger over the photograph, studying the design. You respond to the theme and its rhythms. You love the way pattern and color work together. Perhaps your fingers even itch for the feel of the cloth.

Wonderful. Stop right there. That kind of reaction signals a bonding. If, over the next few days, that quilt continues to satisfy your changing moods, you've found the quilt that is yours for the making.

On the other hand, you may look at the quilt pictures in this book and remain detached. "The branches in Flowering Plum turn and flow gracefully, but the background color . . . ! The delicate appliques in Christmas Star are lovely, but all that white . . . ! The foreground-background interaction in Sweet Dreams is fascinating, but yellow and green . . . ! The design for Peach Blossom is tasteful and simple, but too much pale pastel . . . !" Again and again, the color doesn't quite make it — for you!

So change it. There's nothing sacred about the way the quilts in this book are colored. Color is your medium for personal expression and you can use it to powerful advantage. Your lukewarm reaction to a quilt can be turned into astonished, delighted response when different colors and values are used, emphasizing elements in the pattern that were subdued in the original.

The colors of the quilts in this book reflect the personal preferences of designers Mary Borkowski, Diann Logan, Kathy Sue Guillow and myself. All of us are happy when one from our show of quilts

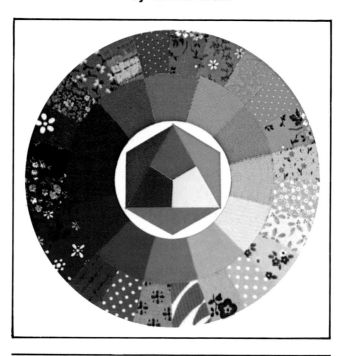

1. A Quilter's Color Wheel

finds an enthusiastic response just as it is. But we are thrilled when someone takes one of our patterns and interprets it with colors of their own choice! That's what quiltmaking is all about. Through this book we are passing our designs on to you; you give them another life. We want our quilt designs to be revitalized continually and to play a part in future dialogues between pattern and quiltmaker.

This is a book of patterns for you to color in your own way, if you wish, and, when the pattern allows, to set in a format of your own devising. No need to panic, however. Mistakes are a necessary part of color exploration but you'll make all your mistakes on paper. Tracing paper, graph paper and colored pens, paints or pencils are quilter's trumps when playing the game of color. And the game comes with a set of convenient theories that show you how to put together winning combinations.

Help for color shy quiltmakers

The color wheel settles all the clear hues of the spectrum into an orderly progression of the basics. It organizes color into harmonious groups and presents quilt designers with a secure foundation for experimentation and elaboration. (See illus. 1.)

The three primary colors are red, yellow and blue. These are the colors from which all other colors derive. The three secondary colors are orange, violet and green. They are created by mixing two primary colors: red and yellow to make orange; red and blue to make violet; blue and yellow to make green. Tertiary colors result from mixing a primary with a secondary color: yellow + orange = yellow-orange; red + orange = red-orange; red + violet = red-violet; blue + violet =

blue-violet; blue + green = blue-green; yellow + green = yellow-green.

These primary, secondary and tertiary colors, arranged in a circle, make up a 12-hue color wheel which could be expanded into a 24-hue color wheel by mixing every two adjacent colors to obtain further intermediate colors. That color wheel could be expanded by mixing pairs of adjacent colors, and so on.

Around the inner circle of fabric solids, the Quilter's Color Wheel (page 59) contains an outer circle of prints classified by dominant color impression and arranged in color wheel sequence.

Every color on the 12-hue color wheel is brilliant and intense, saturated with itself. Each color is absolutely pure, undiminished by the presence of white, black or gray in its formulation. When black, white or gray are mixed with a pure color from the color wheel, tints, tones and shades of that pure color result. (See illus. 2, page 61.)

A tint is produced by mixing a pure color with white. A tone is produced by mixing a pure color with gray. A shade is produced by mixing a pure color with black. The amount of white, gray or black mixed with a pure color creates subtle distinctions within the tints, tones and shades of that color. Every color on the color wheel can be tinted, toned or shaded into a staggering number of variations.

A Quilter's Color Triangle has an equivalent print for every solid (page 61). The dominant color impression of the print corresponds to the value of the solid. For the quiltmaker, every color has two facets: one is the one-color-only fabric, the other is a vari-colored print with a dominant color impression that reflects the color sensation of the one-color-only fabric.

Using the color wheel and the color triangle, groups of colors that relate harmoniously can be isolated into color schemes:

1. No-Color Schemes — white and off-white, and black and white including all the shades of gray in between. In the world of color, black, white and gray are non-colors.

2. One Color Plus Black and/or White — Diann Logan uses a red plus black and white color scheme dramatically in Vanishing Point (page 40).

3. Monochromatic — one color with its tints, tones and shades as the color triangle (page 61) illustrates. Kathy Sue Guillow floats dark blue, medium blue and light blue over a white background to make the Chinese imagery of her Oriental Blossom quilt (page 52).

4. Analogous — two, three or more colors adjacent to each other on the color wheel (see illus. 3-a, page 61). Red, the violets and blue, with printed tonalities of each, back up the spiky white stars that radiate over the surface of Starry Night (page 14).

5. Complementary — any two colors directly opposite each other on the color wheel (see illus. 3-b, page 61). The pink and light green used in Mary Borkowski's Country Rose (page 32) are tints of red and green, a complementary pair of colors on the color wheel.

6. Split Complementary — one color plus the two colors on either side of its complementary color (see illus. 3-c, page 61). The blues, greens and browns of Mary Borkowski's Along the River (page 30) illustrate a split complementary scheme: brown is a deep shade of red-orange; blue and green are the colors on either side of the complement to red-orange (blue-green).

7. Primary or triad — any three colors equidistant from each other on the color wheel (see illus. 3-d, page 61). For a primary color scheme at its boldest, see Mary Borkowski's Sunstar (page 28).

8. Tetrad — four colors equidistant from each other, or four colors, two from either side of a complementary pair of colors (see illus. 3-e & f, page 61). The tetrads are challenging color schemes to coordinate with a pattern or image.

9. Exploratory or Polychrome — without a color wheel category, colors harmonized by the instincts and experimentation of the designer/artist. Quilts composed from pieces of many, sometimes hundreds of different fabrics fall into this category.

A color scheme is beautiful when it harmonizes. A color scheme that is also exciting, stimulating, dynamic, fascinating, moving, alive, vital, surprising, dramatic, interesting, arresting — includes contrast. The relationship of color to color intensifies when contrast is present. For a quiltmaker, contrast is the difference between beautiful-but-dull and beautiful-plus-fertile. Contrast sets up a versus relationship between . . .

Hue and hue — the simplest kind of contrast between undiluted colors as they appear on the color wheel (see Sunstar, page 28).

Light and dark — light, tinted, daylight colors in contrast to heavy, shadowy, nighttime colors (see Flowering Plum, page 18).

Cold and warm — colors from the yellow-orange-red side of the color wheel contrasted to colors from the green-blue-violet side of the color

---

2. A. The Color Triangle formula. B. A Quilter's Color Triangle for red-orange using solid and printed fabrics. C. Further tints, tones and shades of red-orange solid and printed fabrics.

3. Color Schemes: A. Analogous; B. Complementary; C. Split complementary; D. Primary or triad; E. and F. Tetrad. When the shapes in the center of each color wheel are rotated, they point to other combinations within that color scheme.

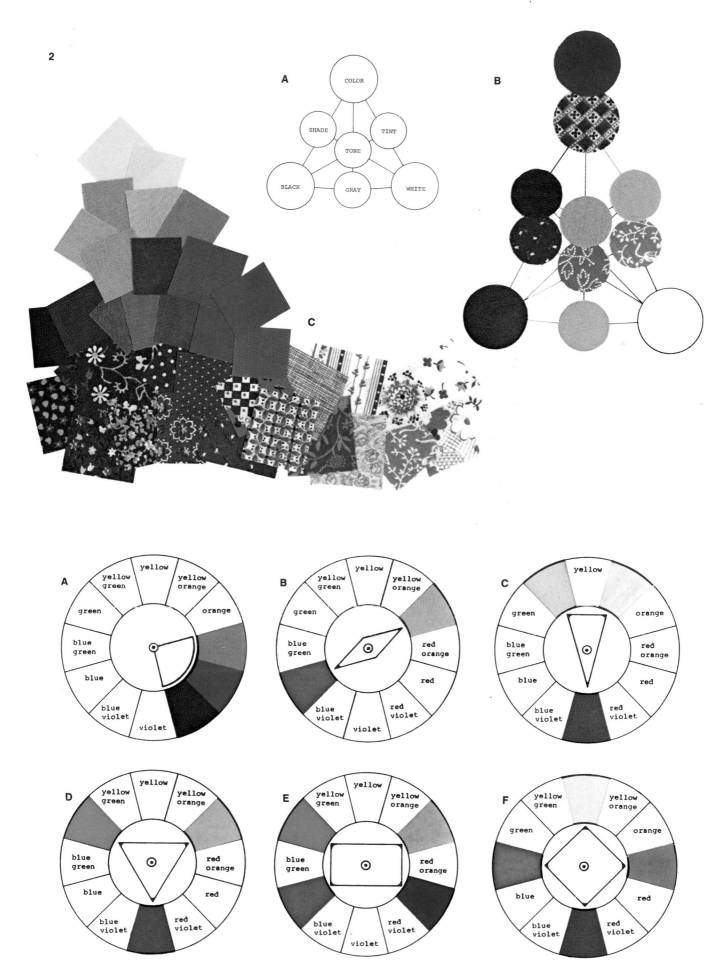

2

A

COLOR

SHADE   TINT

TONE

BLACK   GRAY   WHITE

B

C

A

yellow
yellow green
yellow orange
green
orange
blue green
blue
blue violet
violet

B

yellow
yellow green
yellow orange
green
red orange
blue green
red
blue violet
red violet
violet

C

yellow
green
orange
blue green
red orange
blue
red
blue violet
red violet

D

yellow
yellow green
yellow orange
blue green
red orange
blue
red
blue violet
red violet

E

yellow
yellow green
yellow orange
blue green
red orange
blue violet
red violet
violet

F

yellow green
yellow orange
green
orange
blue
red
blue violet
red violet

61

wheel (see Sweet Dreams, page 44). Cold/warm is an expressive contrast that can suggest, among other effects, nearness and distance (see illus. 4, page 62).

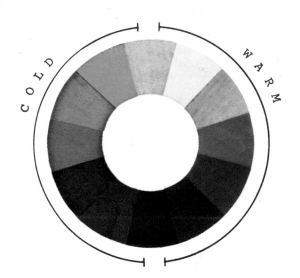

4. The Cold-Warm Contrast: Cold-Warm, shadow-sun, wet-dry, airy-earthy, far-near, relaxing-exciting.

A color and its complement — the eye requires any given color to be balanced by its complement and will spontaneously generate the complement if it's not there. Complements incite each other to maximum brilliance (see Jackie's Tulips, page 34).

Bright and Light — contrast between pure, intense, vivid colors and dull, diluted, thinned colors (see Flowering Plum, page 18).

Size — the contrast between big and little, between the amount of one color in relation to another that allows one color to dominate; a contrast that can modify or intensify the effect of any other contrast (see Hawaiian Fruit Tree, page 22).

Prints and solids — a contrast available to quiltmakers who use fabric as a color vehicle (see Queen's Petticoat and Starry Night, pages 16, 14).

Texture — the contrast between smooth and rough, between dull and shiny, between coarse and fine (see Queen's Petticoat, page 16).

These are the color theories you need to know to play the color game.

The Color Game

The game is defined by the design of the quilt you've chosen to make. If the quilt is composed of one unit repeated over and over (e.g., Sweet Dreams, Joanne's Quilt, Queen's Petticoat), make a copy of that unit, repeated four or six times, by drawing on tracing paper placed over a diagram of the unit in the Quilt Instructions section at the back of the book. If the quilt has an all-over design (e.g., Vanishing Point, Stars Over Hawaii, Oriental Blossom), trace the design onto tracing paper placed over the full-front picture of the quilt in the front of the book. Have photo copies made of your tracing.

While you're copying the design, study the pattern. How many areas or design elements within the pattern need colors of their own in order to be noticed? Which area or element do you want to emphasize with your coloring? Which area or element is secondary? Do you want the background to recede or play an active role? Rate every part of the design on a scale from major to minor.

The color or colors you play with are the ones you love. You throw them into the color wheel like dice and see what happens. List all possible color schemes incorporating your color or colors. Choose the harmony you like the best, the one you feel best suits your design and the purpose for which you're making the quilt. Since color is a visual game, you'll need felt tip pens, paints or colored pencils to see how you're doing. I prefer felt-tip pens because they're easy to apply, blend like paints, and you need to buy only the colors you'll be using from the wide selection offered at art supply stores.

Using the color triangle, adjust the values of all, some, or one of the colors in your scheme. Try one kind of contrast, and another and another. Work toward an effect that sets a tone, expresses a mood or captures an atmosphere you sense lurks within the lines of the the pattern you've traced.

The object of the game is to produce a winning color plan. There's a tried-and-true principle of color distribution that works for your opening move: use small amounts of the brightest, strongest and most intense color or colors in your scheme as accents in limited areas; spread the least intense and most neutral color or colors in your scheme over the largest area and number of pieces. Assign intermediate colors to transition areas or elements within the pattern. Start coloring accordingly.

Remember that light, bright, hot colors advance and stimulate while dark, dull, cool colors recede and relax. Every color will be affected by the color you put next to it. You'll know when one color isn't at its best. Color another version of your pattern, and another, changing the colors around, devising different relationships. Finally, forget the theories and principles and use your instincts. Sometimes the most exciting color plan breaks all the rules to win the game.

If you're very lucky, you can win the color game in one try, but you will most likely have to color version after version of your quilt design before you're pleased. If you can't decide between several approaches, let time help you do the choosing.

Every area that you color represents a fabric, either a solid or a print with a dominant color impression that approximates the color you assign to that area. As you continue to color, you'll develop a sensitivity to a certain area where you feel a print would be appropriate instead of a solid. Or you may decide that you want to interpret every colored area on your plan with an equivalent print.

Illustrations 5 and 6 are color plans for versions of Diann Logan's Joanne's Quilt (page 38) and Mary Borkowski's Country Rose (page 32), created for these make believe situations:

Melissa, whose favorite color is violet these days, wants a quilt for her room. She's 16 years old and full of sparkle and vitality. Violet is a heavy color by itself so it needs the contrast offered by a triad color scheme which includes orange as a warm, light opposite with green as an intermediary between the two. Joanne's Quilt, with its simple but charming repeating pattern composed of squares and triangles, suits a teen-ager's room. On a tracing of six blocks that shows how the pattern and its colors repeat, copied from a diagram in the Quilt Instructions section, three trial colorings are made with felt-tip pen before the fourth and final version captures the desired spirit. (See illus. 5, page 63).

---

5. Color plan for Melissa's Quilt, a version of Diann Logan's Joanne's Quilt, with swatches of the fabrics to be used. Rejected versions, using the violet-green-orange color scheme, are shown to the right.

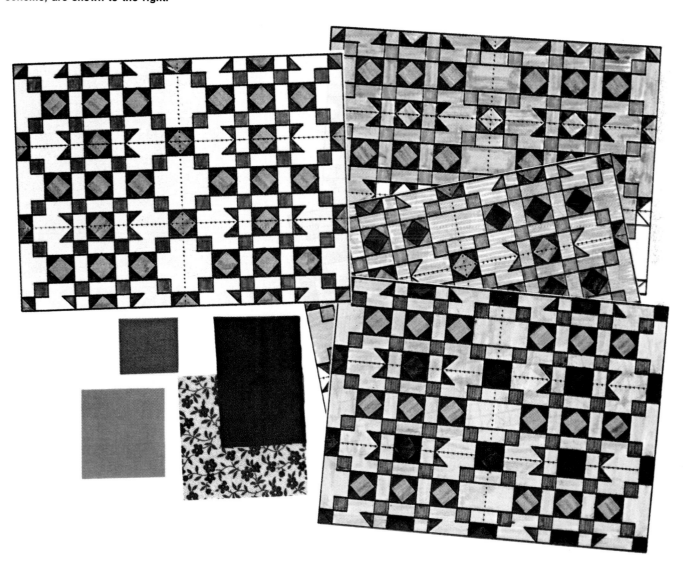

I like the dramatic intensity of the colors the Amish use in their quilts. I also like the neat all-over floral pattern of Mary Borkowski's Country Rose. If Amish colors and Mary's pattern were combined to create a midnight, moonlit impression, how would it look? On a tracing of the entire quilt from the picture on page 147, I filled the background in with black. I decided that I wanted light to slash across the quilt from corner to corner. For the flowers, I used red, blue and yellow full strength in the central moonlit area, changing gradually to the deeper tones of those colors to indicate areas in shadow. Symbolic of foliage, a rich green borders the design. This was one of those rare instances when color, pattern and image worked together perfectly the first time! (See illus. 6.)

Two additional ways to play the color game: (1) Do you have one print in your fabric collection that you're particularly fond of? Use it, and base your color scheme on the colors in the pattern, repeating two or three of the colors in the print in solids or other coordinating prints. The principles of contrast still apply and you'll also need to develop a color plan to discover the most efective distribution of your scheme within the elements of the design. (2) Do you have a large collection of fabric bits and pieces acquired over the years that you would love to use in a quilt? You could translate the designs for Joanne's Quilt and Country Rose into charming, old-fashioned scrap quilts. Separate your scraps by dominant color impression into the reds, blues, greens, yellows, violets, etc. Plan the placement of your prints to move easily from color to color over the surface of the quilt. Above all, an effective scrap quilt is balanced — which requires sensitivity to the total values of every print in relation to its neighbors.

6. Color plan for Midnight Rose, a version of Mary Borkowski's Country Rose, with swatches of the fabrics to be used.

Sensibly Speaking

If you're a beginner, Queen's Petticoat, Joanne's Quilt and Holy Man are easy designs to piece by hand or machine. Peach Blossom or Hawaiian Fruit Trees are reasonable projects to applique if you're trying that hand stitching technique for the first time. If you prefer the speediness of machine construction, all of Diann Logan's designs plus Queen's Petticoat and Starry Night can be pieced by machine, but Vanishing Point and Starry Night are so tricky that you may need the time you save on the machine to get all the pieces into their proper places. Please don't try Christmas Star, Oriental Blossom or Flowering Plum unless you're skilled at appliqueing delicate shapes, and don't attempt Country Rose unless you're willing to stitch all those flowers over and over and over again. If you like pictorial quilting designs, you'll love Peach Blossom, Oriental Blossom and Flowering Plum. If you like to quilt but hate to mark the patterns on the cloth, pieced designs such as Queen's Petticoat, Evolution and Vanishing Point are quilted following the seamlines of the pattern. If you want to challenge your skills, patience and time, Oriental Blossom and Flowering Plum are the quilts for you.

But if you visualize that gorgeous quilt you're going to make adorning the top of your king-sized bed next month when your favorite aunt comes to visit — make a pillow! You'll finish that. Don't let your eyes run away with your knowledge of self. An unfinished quilt tucked away in a closet is a nag, or time and money wasted, or a frustrating experience, none of which will do you a bit of good.

The Size Question

There are two points of view about the size of a quilt. There are those who feel that the quilt takes priority over where it's going to live, and then there are those who measure the bed or space and design to fit.

The quilt-comes-first people believe that a quilt is a work of art and must therefore be designed for its own sake with aesthetic considerations foremost. If they find an antique quilt with an especially attractive design, they buy it first and then look for a bed or wall space to show it off. Designers of this persuasion create quilts that end up a certain size because that's how the design worked out. At most they may take into account the size of the top of a mattress, making certain that it's covered, but leaving the overhang to the demands of the design.

The bed-or-space-comes-first people are the practical ones. They measure and then shop or create to fill those dimensions. They use mattress measurements to determine the size of the primary design area of the quilt. They measure the height of the bed to determine quilt overhang, and the secondary design area of the quilt.

To customize a quilt for a particular bed or other space, there's no substitute for on-site measurement. Mattress sizes may be standardized, but the distance from top of mattress to floor varies with the kind of bed, and also changes when a dust ruffle or other decorative device takes up some of the distance. A comparison of mattress measurements with the overall sizes of the quilts in this volume indicates what size mattress each quilt will cover, with how much to spare (illus. 7).

7.

Picture			in inches	
Page	QUILT	Size	Mattress Size	
			crib	- 27 x 50
16	Queen's Petticoat (wall)	56 x 80		
56	American Indian	64 x 82		
18	Flowering Plum	78 x 86	studio	- 30 x 75
38	Joanne's Quilt	80 x 80		
16	Queen's Petticoat (bed)	80 x 92		
28	Sunstar	83 x 100	twin	- 39 x 75
22	Hawaiian Fruit Trees	87 x 111		
30	Along the River	88 x 92	wide	
40	Vanishing Point	90 x 90	twin	- 48 x 75
42	Evolution	90 x 90		
44	Sweet Dreams	90 x 90		
48	Symphony in F	90 x 90	double	- 54 x 75
14	Starry Night	92 x 100		
26	Christmas Star	92 x 100		
52	Oriental Blossom	92 x 108	queen	- 60 x 80
46	Holy Man	96 x 96		
34	Jackie's Tulips	96 x 99		
24	Stars Over Hawaii	99 x 99	king	- 72 x 84
32	Country Rose	104 x 120		
54	Peach Blossom	108 x 110		

Suppose your chosen quilt isn't big enough. You can make the quilt as designed and display it over a solid color spread that hangs the desired length, or you can enlarge the quilt to fit.

Making the border wider enlarges a quilt. With the exception of Peach Blossom and Flowering Plum, all the quilts in this book can be widened and lengthened by adding a border or two or three. (The nature of the designs and the rounded corners of Peach Blossom and Flowering Plum make bordering these quilts difficult.) You'll need to add 8 to 10 inches to the length of a quilt you want to cover the pillows on a bed with extra to tuck under. Oriental Blossom (page 52) was designed with this purpose in mind.

Quilts such as Queen's Petticoat, Sweet Dreams, Evolution, Country Rose and Flowering Plum are composed of small repeating design units, called **blocks in quilter's language. These quilts can be** enlarged by adding extra rows of blocks; they can also be reduced by deleting rows of blocks. If the size of a block is 12 x 12 inches, and a row is added to one side and the top, both the length and width of the quilt will be increased by 12 inches; if the size of a block is 14 x 14 inches the quilt's size will be increased by 14 inches in each direction, and so on. A quilt can be enlarged by adding both blocks and borders. It's always wise to plan enlargements or reductions on graph paper.

Enlarging a quilt affects yardage requirements. To decide how much extra material you'll need for a border: (1) add the length to all four borders; (2) divide that total figure by the width of the fabric; (3) multiply that answer by the width of the border; and (4) you have the answer.

total border length (inches)	÷	fabric width (inches)	×	border width (inches)	=	Border Fabric Needed (inches)

Example: 360″ ÷ 45″ = 8 x 3½″ = 28″.

If you're adding blocks: (1) Count the total number of pieces (squares, triangles, appliques, etc.) you need to cut from one fabric; (2) divide that total by the number of pieces you can cut in a row across the width of the fabric (to make it easy for yourself, draw it out on graph paper or draw it actual size on a piece of paper as long as the width of the fabric); (3) multiply that answer by the depth, or inches of fabric, you'll need for one row; and (4) that's the amount of fabric you'll need.

total # of pieces to be cut	÷	# of pieces in row across fabric width	×	depth (inches) of 1 row	=	Fabric Needed (inches) For Pieces

Example: 104 ÷ 12 = 8.67 or 9 x 4½″ = 40½″.

You'll need to repeat your calculations for every fabric. Always add a safety measure to your total!

Enlarging your quilt will also affect batting size and the amount of fabric you'll need for the lining.

Decisions in the Fabric Store

With your color plan or quilt picture in one hand and a list of the fabric yardages you'll need in the other, you're ready to begin the hunt for that perfect color and appropriate print. Close your eyes to everything but the colors you're going to use. Separate all likely candidates from those that are impossible. Take them to an area where you can see them without interference from other distracting colors. If you're in a place where the lighting is fluorescent, try to look at the fabric under daylight or incandescent light (fluorescent distorts color).

Group fabrics that will be stitched together next to each other. Stand back to judge how they work as a unit, referring to your color plan or picture for the tonalities you're trying to match. Remem-

ber that you're gauging a print by its dominant color impression, something that you can't do with it right under your nose. Try other combinations.

If you're lucky you'll find every fabric in one place, but chances are you'll be dissatisfied in some instances, so buy what you need of what you're certain you want and move on to the next shop with samples in hand. Choosing solids and prints that materialize your image may require lots of patience, especially if you're looking for **twelve coordinating fabrics to make a Starry Night quilt,** and it will exercise your color sensitivity, but having that color plan or picture for reference will keep your purchases on the mark.

Prints with tiny figures in a close repeat have always been favored by quiltmakers because they blend, they don't call attention to themselves except by plan. Viewed from a distance their patterns and colors blur into a dominant color impression that can be handled as a tonality in a color scheme. Handsome quilts have been created using only prints carefully chosen to give the impression of a tint, tone or shade of a particular color. Prints with large motifs in contrasting colors are aggressive and difficult to control within the harmony of a fabric color scheme.

Manufacturers, recognizing the special needs of quiltmakers, have produced an enormous variety of miniature prints lately. When they create coordinating collections of prints, they inject variety into the medley with contrast between prints that are geometric in nature and prints that are figurative; with contrast between densely patterned prints and prints with more solid background area showing between motifs, sometimes on a background of pin dots or checks; with contrast between prints colored in a closely related selection of hues and prints with colors that are spaced out on the color wheel. You can apply these variations when organizing your own coordinating collection of prints (illus. 8). Keep

8.

A coordinated set of printed patterns.

a firm grasp on the dominant color impression you want each print to communicate, discipline your color sensitivity, and much uncertainty will be eliminated.

Must you buy that 100% cotton fabric that's expensive when the print that's 30% polyester is just as nice and less expensive? Do you have to take the 100% cotton solid that's not quite as perfect as the 60% polyester solid which you prefer? When the percentage of polyester in a fiber blend exceeds 50%, the possibility of bearding increases (bearding happens when the polyester fibers in batting merge and creep through the polyester fibers in the fabric — after a quilt is made and in use!). Tough polyester fibers present resistance to the hand-guided needle which is disturbing when hand quilting even if the the quilt top is machine assembled. Pressing a quilt block with polyester blends stitched to all-cottons poses problems because cotton requires a hot setting which wreaks havoc on polyester. Unless you're extremely patient and experienced, polyester blends are frustrating to applique because the material doesn't hold a crease. For all these reasons, plus the sometimes snobbish reason that "it's natural," quiltmakers prefer to use 100% cotton whenever possible. However, if that print or solid that's exactly right for your quilt contains 33% or less polyester in its makeup, I'd buy it if I were you.

Finishes such as permanent press, soil resistance, etc. toughen the fibers of cottons and cotton blends. Mary Borkowski specifies sheets for linings in her directions, but some quiltmakers find that sheets, which usually have such special finishes, make hand quilting tiring to do. Test on samples to determine your own reaction.

If you're making a quilt for display, one that won't be subjected to wear and tear and that will be dry cleaned when and if it's required, you can indulge in a mix of fibers and textures. Otherwise, keep all your fabrics water washable. Don't buy fabric that's coarse and heavy, or flimsy and loosely woven, or stiff. Fabrics for hand quilting should feel soft and pliable when scrunched up in your hand. Lining material in particular should be soft and lightweight, and easy for the quilting needle to pierce.

You, the quilt you're making, and posterity deserve the finest quality fabric you can find. Quiltmakers, individualists in fabric preference as in everything else, all vehemently agree on that.

The Nuts and Bolts

Now's the time to check your basic equipment. A good steam iron and padded board. A sewing machine that's clean, oiled, and in top working condition. A round quilting hoop, about 23 inches in diameter or a quilting frame that's complete down to the last screw.

If you don't have a sharp dressmaker's scissors that rests easily in your hand, buy one immediately because you'll be using it a lot to cut all that gorgeous fabric. You'll also need a paper cutting scissors (never cut paper with the scissors you use for fabric!), and a small scissors for cutting out tiny appliques and clipping threads while you sew. To make those precision-cut templates so essential for perfect piecework, you'll need a razor-bladed utility knife or an X-Acto® knife, and a steel-edged ruler.

Handsewing needles are graded by numbers; the higher the number, the finer the needle. General sewing needles are called sharps. They are long and slender with small eyes which distinguish them from embroidery needles which have elongated eyes. Quilting needles, also called betweens, are short and stumpy. Buy needles packaged in assorted sizes to try so that you can discover what suits your fingers, your fabric and your style the best. Buy one of those little needle threaders while you're at it. And be sure you have a thimble. Even if you've never gotten used to using one, you'll appreciate the protection once you've started sewing on a quilt!

If you intend to piece by machine, buy several packages of needles in the size recommended for cotton. Choose good quality cotton-wrapped polyester thread colored to match the predominant colors of the fabrics you'll be sewing. For hand-sewing, 100% cotton thread, No. 50, is favored over cotton-wrapped polyester but it's sometimes hard to find. Polyester thread tends to twist and knot while handsewing, but the tendency can be corrected by waxing each length of thread you cut. Avoid those bargain spools of polyester thread which twist and knot to an irritating degree.

Quilting thread is different from sewing thread, heavier, and always 100% cotton. Buy that to blend into the fabric colors you'll be quilting, unless contrasting thread is specified for a particular effect as in Mary Borkowski's Christmas Star. Choose a tone that's darker over one that's lighter if you have a choice. Because of its extra strength and manageability, some quiltmakers use quilting thread for everything — piecing, appliqueing and quilting.

Check the Quilter's Shopping List for other items you don't have and may need (illus. 9). The

9.

Quilter's Shopping List

sections which follow will explain the how's and why's. And if you haven't read the instructions for the particular quilt you're making, do so now. You may be surprised by some of the methods and techniques employed by the designers who made the original quilts.

That Enlarging Chore

Nobody likes enlarging. Even those who do it easily consider it a necessary evil. Look at it this way: besides providing the patterns without which you would have to choose another design, enlarging is like a rehearsal for the main event. Since every line you draw represents a seam you'll be stitching, you're solving problems before they arise.

To get on with the task as quickly and efficiently as possible, get some graph paper that's already marked off into 1-inch squares. You can buy it in 25 x 38-inch sheets (see Resources, page 190) that are more than adequate for every pattern in this book except Stars Over Hawaii, for which you'll have to tape several sheets together. But if you suddenly decide to do the job at midnight when the stores are closed, take a large grocery bag, cut it open on the side seam and around the bottom, trim it neatly and iron it flat. With a red felt tip pen measure and rule a grid of 1-inch squares on the clean side of the bag.

If you draw a vertical line down the center of the pattern you're enlarging, are the outlines on either side of the line mirror images of each other? If so, you'll only have to enlarge one side. If you draw another line horizontally across the center of the original, are the four sections between the lines identical? If so, you only need to enlarge one fourth of the design.

1. Starting at one corner on the original, number the horizontal and vertical lines that cross the portion of the design you need to enlarge.

2. Duplicate that numbering on your 1-inch graph paper. If you're only enlarging a portion of the design, rule horizontal and vertical lines on your 1-inch graph paper that correspond in position to the lines on the original.

3. With a contrasting colored pen, make a dot on the original at each point where a grid line intersects a design outline.

4. Copy those dots onto your 1-inch grid paper, making sure that the dots are on the properly numbered line, in a position that corresponds to the position on the original. To avoid confusion, follow the outline of each pattern piece to its conclusion. (When design outlines are complicated, additional ½-inch lines between the 1-inch lines give you more reference points. Make these lines a different color on both the original and the enlargement.)

5. Connect the dots on your 1-inch grid with lines that are similar in character to the lines of the original. If lines are straight, draw against a ruler. If the design includes perfect circles, use a compas or try to find something round you can trace. And draw in pencil with an eraser handy.

6. Compare the shapes you've drawn to the shapes on the original. Correct any awkward out-

lines, lines that are wiggly, too curved or not curved enough, or otherwise inaccurate.

7. Cut out the enlargement. If you've only enlarged a portion of the design, trace the outline of your enlargement onto folded paper and cut out the full-size pattern.

8. Identify each pattern with the name of the quilt and any other information you need to know for the future. (Illus. 10 a-d.)

Templates

Before you use any of the actual size geometric patterns (squares, triangles, rectangles, etc.) printed in this book, check them for accuracy. Or better yet, make a set of your own geometric patterns for piecing using graph paper or an artist's angle, following the measurements stated in the Instruction Section.

Accuracy is essential for perfect pieced patchwork and accuracy begins with your patterns. Patterns that don't fit together precisely will cause a snowballing succession of problems later. Patterns that are even a little bit too large or too small, when that difference is multiplied, change the size of a quilt. Since all the pieced quilts in this book can be stitched by machine, the patterns given may include a standard ¼-inch seam allowance. But if you prefer stitching by hand, make your patterns without seam allowances so that the outside of the pattern is your stitching line.

Templates are quiltmaker's working patterns. The original patterns you make on paper are reference patterns to be filed away for use when you need to replace a template or check the accuracy of a template you've used over and over again. (Stars Over Hawaii is the exception: for that quilt the paper pattern is the working pattern as well.)

To make a set of templates for piecing: On sturdy cardboard, preferably artist's illustration board, trace an exact duplicate of your set of paper patterns. Holding a razor-bladed utility knife or X-Acto® knife against a steel-edged ruler to assure a perfectly straight cut, cut out each template on the outline you traced. If the cardboard is strong, cardboard templates for pieced patchwork should survive the making of one quilt.

To make a set of applique templates: Since applique templates are usually curvy rather than straight edged, use a lighter weight cardboard that can be cut with scissors for templates. Trace the outline of each pattern onto the cardboard and cut out through the center of the line you traced. For very small shapes a fingernail scissors is easier to use than a larger scissors. When you've finished cutting out the cardboard template, use sandpaper or an emery board to smooth the contours where necesary. If you'll be cutting many pieces from your applique template, as you will if you are making Country Rose, make several templates to start because pencil tracing friction will wear down one template before you've

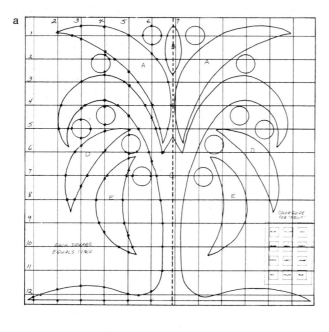

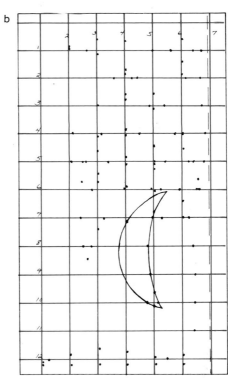

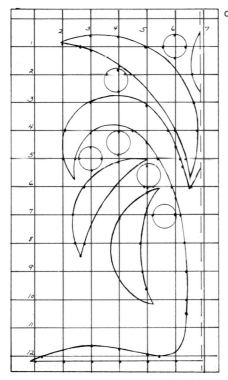

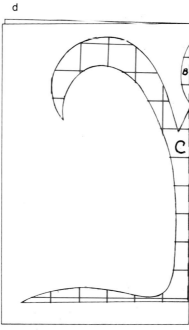

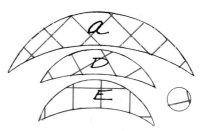

10. Enlarging the pattern for Stars Over Hawaii: a. original with central dotted line separating identical halves of the design, grid lines numbered, and dots where grid line and pattern intersect. **b.** enlargement with grid lines numbered, dots copied and one pattern piece outlined. **c.** finished enlargement with lines connecting all dots. Before cutting, a copy is made to be used as a guide for placing appliques on the background fabric. **d.** cut out patterns with B and C ready to be cut from folded paper into full-size patterns. Since circles are identical, only one pattern is required.

finished cutting all the pieces. Note: applique templates never include seam allowances.

To make a special set of piecing or applique templates that are a pleasure to use: laminate a sheet or sheets of ordinary fine sandpaper to one side of your cardboard with white glue. Dry overnight under pressure. Cut your templates from the sandpaper surfaced board. When using these templates, the sandpaper surface "grabs" the fabric, preventing the template from moving and the fabric from slipping while the outlines of the template are being traced onto the cloth.

Templates made from heavy clear acetate, which can be purchased at art supply stores, are useful when you need to center a design on the fabric in the middle of every piece you cut, or when you need to align the edges of the piece you're cutting with lines in the print of the fabric. Fix stars or circles of colored sticky tape to the acetate so that you can find the template when you need it. Quilting templates are discussed on page 87.

Picture Page	The Pieced Quilts	Picture Page	The Appliqued Quilts
	A pieced quilt is made by sewing small, specially shaped pieces of fabric together to make larger pieces of fabric, creating a pattern with the process.		An appliqued quilt is made by sewing smaller, specially shaped pieces of fabric onto larger pieces of fabric, creating a design with the process.
42	Evolution	30	Along the River
46	Holy Man	26	Christmas Star
38	Joanne's Quilt	32	Country Rose
16	Queen's Petticoat	18	Flowering Plum
14	Starry Night	22	Hawaiian Fruit Tree
44	Sweet Dreams	34	Jackie's Tulips
48	Symphony in F	52	Oriental Blossom
40	Vanishing Point	54	Peach Blossom
		24	Stars Over Hawaii

AMERICAN INDIAN (pg. 56) and SUNSTAR (pg. 28) are made using a combination of both techniques.

Cutting

This is the last chance you'll have to get that final bit of shrinkage out of your fabrics and to find out whether their dyes will live together compatibly without one staining the others because of fading. Toss the lot into your washer and dryer. While you're waiting, re-read the cutting and assembly instructions for the quilt you're making. Check them against the full-front picture of the quilt and any drawings in the Instruction Section. Be sure you understand what goes where, how and why lest you spend time cutting pieces you can't use!

Press with a steam iron, returning any fabrics that are off-grain to the state where threads parallel to the selvedge (the straight grain) are consistently perpendicular (90° angle) to the threads running from selvedge to selvedge (the cross grain). Tug the material across the bias of the fabric to set it to rights (see illus. 12).

Spread your fabric full width on a table. A surface that's covered with felt or flannel will keep the material from sliding around. If you're limber enough for floor cutting, a rug will do the same. I like to cut while standing so I use an ironing board.

Since quiltmakers cut on or around outlines which have been marked on the fabric, you'll need pencils that make lines you can see. For a quilt that varies from dark to light that means several pencils, white, pink, light blue or what-ever color will show distinctly on dark fabrics, and regular pencils with leads from semi-soft to hard for other fabrics. On light, pale fabrics use a hard artist's pencil; it can't make dark smudgy lines that will shadow through to the outside after sewing and it won't soil matching thread sewn on a pencil-marked line. All pencils must be capable of holding a very sharp point, eliminating tailor's chalk and very soft leads. You'll need a little pencil sharpener to keep leads pointed.

Pieces to be stitched together by machine need to be cut from templates that include the standard ¼-inch seam allowance. The line that is traced around the template onto the wrong side of the fabric is the cutting line (see illus. 13).

Pieces that are to be stitched together by hand need to be cut from templates that do not include any seam allowance. The line that is traced onto the wrong side of the fabric from the template is the sewing line (see illus. 14).

Place your template in position at the top of your fabric right next to the selvedge, sandpaper side down if you've given it a clutching surface. Don't include the selvedge in any of the pieces you're cutting; it tends to draw its edge. Hold the template firmly with one hand while you trace its outlines with a pencil. Tuck the sharp point of the pencil against the edge of the template and draw around all sides with quick, smooth strokes. If you have to scrub the fabric with your pencil to make a line you can see, you've got the

12. Fabric terminology and a block for Evolution stitched with grainlines of each piece running parallel to the sides of the block, as they would if the block were one piece of fabric.

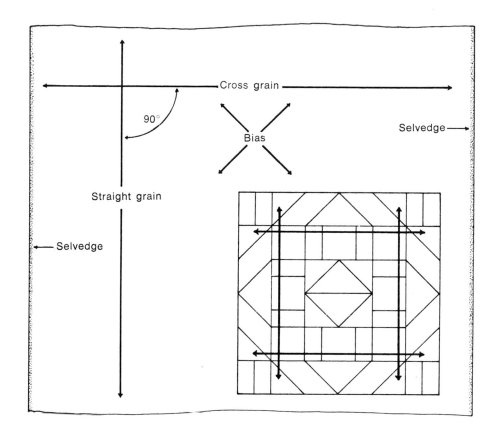

Cross grain

90°

Bias

Selvedge

Straight grain

Selvedge

13. Fabric marked for cutting using templates for machine piecing.

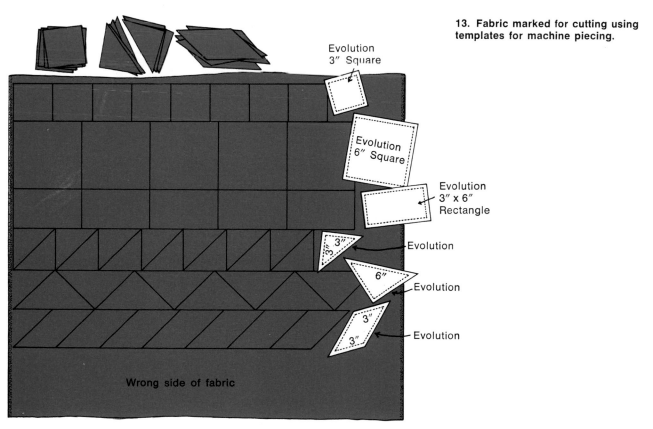

Evolution
3" Square

Evolution
6" Square

Evolution
3" x 6"
Rectangle

Evolution

Evolution

Evolution

Wrong side of fabric

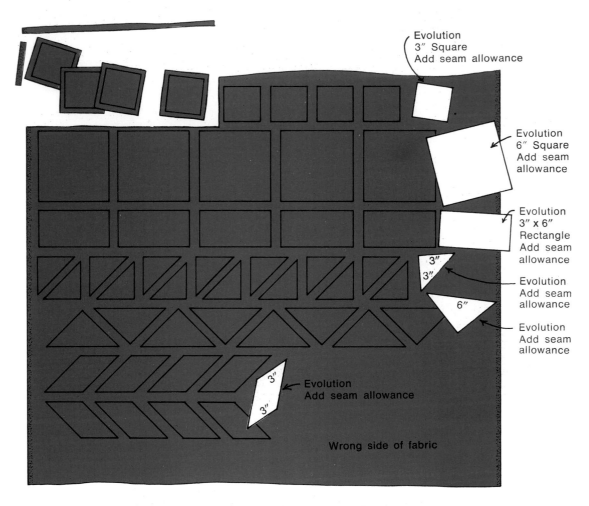

14. Fabric marked for cutting using templates for hand piecing.

wrong pencil. Move the template over next to the outline you've just pencilled and trace another piece. Continue until you've made a row of outlines across the width of the fabric. The lower edge of your outlines will be even if you've followed a thread line across the fabric, or you can begin by ruling a line that follows the grain from side to side and matching your template to that line.

If you're marking outlines for a quilt to be machine-sewn, adjacent pieces will share an outline (see illus. 13). If you're making outlines for handsewing, outlines must be ½ inch apart, allowing for a ¼-inch seam allowance around each piece (see illus. 14). I use a "rule of forefinger" to gauge the distance in between, making outlines an index finger's width apart. Find a finger that's ½ inch wide if your forefinger isn't.

Watch your pencil point. When it blunts, sharpen it. A blunt lead will force the line you draw away from the edge of the template, enlarging the shape. Even that slight enlargement, when multi-

plied, and when you try to stitch enlarged pieces to exact-size pieces, will cause problems that will try your perseverance. When you have finished marking for cutting, every outline should be an exact duplicate of the template, and every piece should be an exact duplicate of every other piece.

Align the edges of square and rectangular templates against the straight and cross grains of the fabric. To determine which edge of triangles and rhomboids should be "on the straight," look at a diagram of the block you're constructing. When the block is entirely stitched together, the grain of all pieces should be in the vertical-horizontal relationship of unseamed fabric (see illus. 12, page 71). Quilts that include diamonds, hexagons, or irregular shapes in their piecework are exceptions to this rule; in such cases the longest edge of the template is aligned to the straight of the fabric, or the quiltmaker plans so that a bias edge will be seamed to a straight edge. With the exception of Starry Night, which has patterns marked for straight of grain, all the pieced quilts in this book are cut according to the rule.

Printed fabrics may show cause for another exception to the rule. If you're cutting pieces from striped or checked fabric, align the edges of the template with the lines of the fabric's pattern, not with the threads in the fabric, otherwise your finished quilt will look tipsy in certain places.

Reverse the template for half the rhomboid shapes cut from patterned material and, for hand piecing, half the rhomboid shapes cut from solid fabric as well. These pieces need reversing to fit into a block for Evolution (see illus. 15). Many of the odd-shaped pieces for Starry Night also require template reversing when patterned fabric is used.

To speed the cutting of regular geometric shapes, cut the fabric into strips as wide as the

15. Arrows point to rhomboids that need reversing to fit the plan of the design.

depth of a row, and then chop the strips into pieces on or between the pencilled lines. Exactly on the pencilled lines if you're cutting for machine-sewing because you'll be using the edge you cut as a guide for seaming. If the edge slants, dips or waves, so will your seam, and that will cause another succession of problems. For handsewing pieces, cut in between the pencilled lines regularly and evenly, not because it's required, but because it's good craftsmanship and because it's easier to sew pieces together when seam allowances are the same size.

Tracing and cutting for applique is done on the right side of the fabric. Very small applique templates can be positioned on the fabric without regard for fabric grain, but when templates become larger, they should be placed identically with the grain (e.g., the petal shapes for Country Rose) or they should be arranged so that the grain, when the section is constructed, runs north/ south and east/west (e.g., the pieces for Along the River) (see illus. 16).

Applique templates never include seam allowances. The lines you draw on the face of the fabric are the turn-under lines, so they should be faintly visible but not so dark that you'll have trouble concealing them when sewing. When cutting, stay an even distance outside the outline, allowing ⅛-inch seam allowance for small appliques or appliques with complex contours and ¼-inch seam allowance for larger appliques with simple shapes.

To cut bias strips to be appliqued into curving lines, rule lines the specified distance apart and as long as necessary diagonally across the bias of the fabric (see illus 16). For long bias strips, use the method described for cutting bias binding on page 93.

Appliques for Stars Over Hawaii and Christmas Star are cut on folded fabric as described in the directions for those quilts.

Measure and rule the outlines of large squares, rectangles, and long strips for which no patterns are provided on the reverse side of the fabric, carefully following the grain. These pieces can be torn instead of cut but tearing tends to throw the grain of the fabric off and you have to contend with fuzzy edges and yards of drooling threads as well.

Before you cut, determine whether the measurements given in the directions include seam allowances or not. Instructions that read "cut a 14x14-inch square (finished size)" mean the square will be 14 x 14 inches after sewing, and imply that you must cut a square 14½ x 14½ inches to include a ¼-inch seam allowance on all sides. When cutting strips for borders, you'll need to add a ¼-inch seam allowance at both ends and sides if the measurements in the instructions don't include seam allowances, and a seam allowance where you have to sew two strips together to make up the required length.

Large background squares and borders will be pieced together with right sides facing, even if they are part of an appliqued top. A sewing line ¼ inch inside the cutting line, on the reverse side of the fabric, helps assure that all important accuracy — accuracy — accuracy!

Piecing the Blocks

Place a picture of the quilt you're making or your color plan and the designer's directions where you can refer to them easily. Be ready with plenty of pins, a thread clipping scissors, and set up an ironing board with iron nearby. Set the stitching gauge on your sewing machine for 12 to 15 stitches per inch, and adjust the tension to produce a tight, firm seam. Tiny stitches, although more difficult to unpick if you make a mistake, resist pulling apart at start and finish. Arrange the fabric pieces for one block face up, in position as you will be sewing them together.

Every pieced block design is a little puzzle. With the exception of Starry Night, the pieced quilts in this book are designed on a grid of

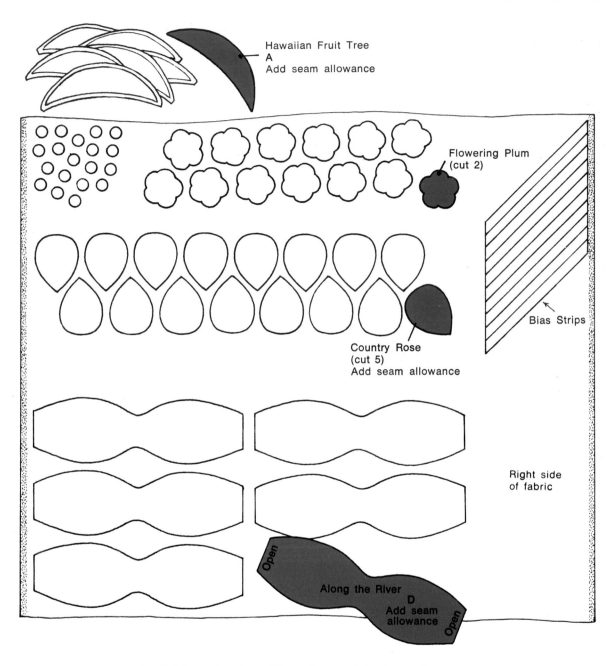

Hawaiian Fruit Tree
A
Add seam allowance

Flowering Plum
(cut 2)

Bias Strips

Country Rose
(cut 5)
Add seam allowance

Right side
of fabric

Open

Along the River
D
Add seam
allowance

Open

16. Fabric marked for cutting using templates for applique.

squares. Each block can be subdivided into square or rectangular segments, and those segments can be subdivided further into basic pairs or triplets (see illus. 17). Vanishing Point, although designed on a grid of squares, is assembled according to its own rules as if it were one huge block (see instructions, page 156). The directions for Starry Night show how each of those blocks is assembled (page 99).

Start by sewing together all the pairs and triplets in your block. Pick up two adjacent pieces, flopping one over the other with right sides fac-

ing, and pin them together next to the edges you'll be seaming. Match the cut edges exactly. If you're sewing a square and a rectangle together in any combination, match the corners exactly as well (see illus. 18-d & e). But if one or both of the pieces you'll be seaming together is a triangle or rhomboid, there's a slight hitch.

Go back to your original paper patterns with the dotted lines that indicate seam lines. On triangles and rhomboids, pierce holes into the corners where seamlines turn. Align the edges of two paper patterns, one or both a triangle or

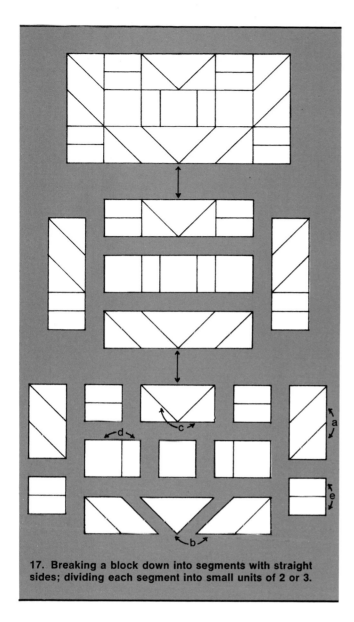

17. Breaking a block down into segments with straight sides; dividing each segment into small units of 2 or 3.

from the cut edge. A straight seam, not one that wobbles. One that's consistently ¼ inch inside the edge of the fabric. When you've finished, trim the thread at either end leaving a ½-inch tail for insurance against unravelling.

Open the pieces you just stitched together with right sides up. Do the edges on either side of the seam meet precisely and continue smoothly on their way? Yes? Hooray! (See illus. 18).

At the ironing board turn all your rows upside down. Seam allowances on pieced blocks are pressed closed to one side. At points where three, four or more seam allowances will converge, they can clump into a hard lump unless pressed in alternate directions. It's impossible to avoid some seam allowance buildup when machine piecing, but it can be minimized by pressing one seam to the right and one seam to the left when you know that in a future seam those seams will meet.

One exception that takes precedence: press seam allowances away from light colored fabrics over the darker fabrics adjacent. Do that first, then press the other seam allowances to one side or the other as you judge best (see illus. 19). Turn and press each row from the top, making sure that every seam is open as far as it will go.

You can't stitch rows of piecework together accurately unless the rows are pinned together accurately first. Locate the seams that will run into one another when stitched together. Insert a pin through the thread of one seam into the thread of the opposite seam; holding firmly, re-insert the pin into the fabric below the seam and bring it out. If both of these crucial seams are straight there's no problem, but if one of the seams is angled, pierce that seam at a point ¼ inch down from the edge. That's where the new seam will cross (see illus. 20-a).

Where many seam allowances converge, slanting the pin into the fabric below the seam may move the edges off alignment. In that case, stab the converging seams together with a perpendicular pin and, holding firmly, insert another pin to the side.

After pinning all crucial seams together, pin in between as often as you feel you'll need to keep the edges matching properly (see illus. 20-b). If you discover that one piece mysteriously shrunk or stretched from the size it's supposed to be, you can ease the two together by distributing the slack material between spaced pins, or you can stretch the area between your hands as it is being stitched. Sew the segments together ¼ inch from the edge, moving slowly when you cross a pin to avoid sharp impact that could snap the needle. Your machine needle will occasionally glance off a pin and the point will blunt, but the sacrifice of needles is worth the result of careful and extensive pinning — seams that run into each other and cross precisely, just as they do on the diagram of the block (see illus. 21).

rhomboid, as if you were going to sew them together. Match the holes. Notice that one or both of the patterns' corners refuse to match. That's the correct position for sewing (see illus. 18-a, b & c).

At first it may help to mark the reverse side of your fabric pieces with dots to match up, but your eye will quickly become accustomed to pairing these pieces with just the right amount of overlap. The point where two pattern outlines intersect should be ¼ inch in from the outside edge; you'll start and finish seaming at that tiny intersection.

Stick a length of colored tape to the plate of the sewing machine ¼ inch to the right of the needle. Even if the plate on your sewing machine is incised with lines that indicate depth of seam allowance, the colored tape line is easier to see. Matching the cut edges of the pieces you're sewing to the seam allowance guide, sew a straight seam from one end to the other exactly ¼ inch

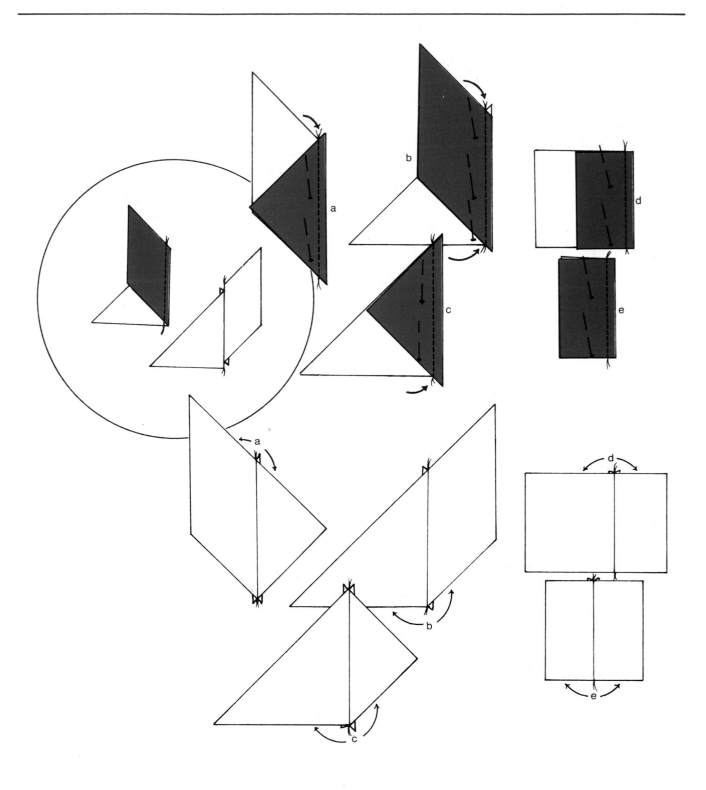

18. a, b & c. Triangles and rhomboids stitched correctly with arrows pointing to corners that meet but don't match. Circled illustrations show what happens when pieces are improperly aligned. d and e. Rectangles and squares, with corners and edges matching, stitched together properly.

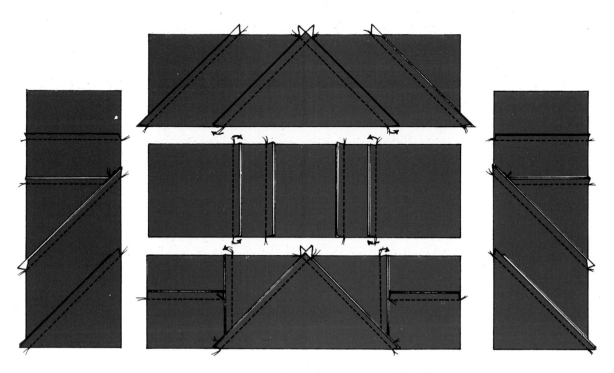

19. Strips with seam allowances pressed closed, to
one side, alternated to minimize seam allowance
build-up.

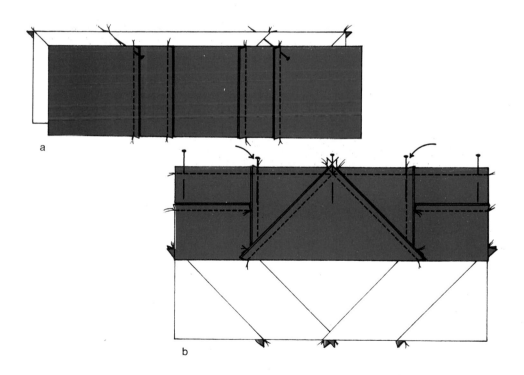

a

b

20. a. Pinning crucial seams-that-must-match together
before sewing. Pins are stabbed through each seam
¼ inch below the cut edge. b. Two strips seamed
together with arrows pointing to the crucial seams.

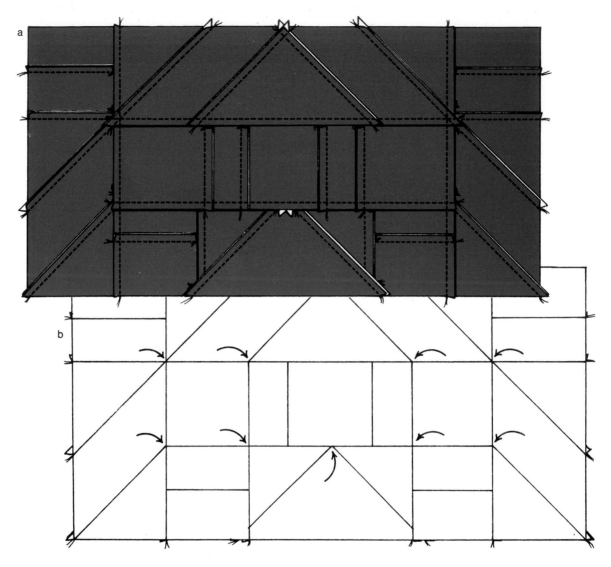

21. a. Machine pieced block with seam allowances pressed closed. b. Front of block with arrows pointing to seams that meet and match precisely on line.

When the block is assembled, press the long seam allowances flat, to one side, with an up and down rather than sliding movement of the iron to avoid ruffling previously pressed seam allowances. Turn the block over and press from the top using a damp cloth. Clip or pull out stray threads that have wandered through the seams.

The first block you make is your prototype. With it you solved problems of construction and pressing for all the blocks that follow. Pin it up where you can refer to it. Use assembly line tactics to speed making the rest of the blocks. Sew all similar pairs for each block at the same time, chaining them together without stopping to cut the thread between seams (see illus. 22).

If you're thinking that all this machine sewing of a quilt is sacrilegious to the purity of the product, that a handsewn quilt has aesthetic values a machine-pieced quilt doesn't possess, that tradition must be served with miles of tiny running stitches, you're thinking nonsense, if you'll forgive my being so blunt. Women used to make quilts by hand because they had no other choice, and when they had the choice they grabbed it, continuing handwork only when necessary or because they loved to do it. Quiltmaking continues to thrive and grow because it assimilates new tools, methods and changing ideas of color and design. If you dislike sitting for long periods at a whirring machine, preferring instead the peaceful, gentle rhythm of handsewing, that's the only reason you need for piecing your quilt by hand.

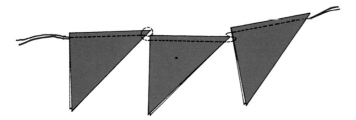

22. Chaining to speed the machine-stitching of similar pieces.

Hand piecing is portable. You can take it anywhere. It's easier for beginners to piece accurately if they sew by hand. When hand piecing, you match the sewing lines pencilled on the back of each piece of fabric. You follow the pencilled line with your needle, assuring a straight seam. You sew from the beginning to the end of a pencilled line, not into the seam allowances. You never sew the seam allowances of previous seams down but leave them free. Because seam allowances aren't secured, you can press them in different directions to avoid clumping.

Pinning is just as essential to precise hand piecing as it is to precise machine piecing. With the right sides of the fabric facing, pin together the pencilled corners that mark the beginning and end of a seam, checking both pieces to see that the pin emerges at the proper point (see illus. 23). Then add pins in between, still pinning the pencilled lines together. To avoid stabbing the handsewer, point the pins up or down.

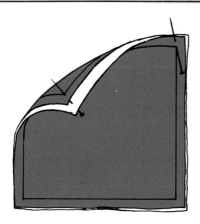

23. For hand piecing, joining pencilled seamlines of two pieces with a start and stop pin.

Thread your sewing needle with about 18 inches of single thread, knotting the end you cut from the spool. Longer thread tends to knot and wear thin. Waxing the thread with beeswax or paraffin gives it strength and prevents tangles. Starting at one corner, make a series of evenly spaced,

small, in-and-out stitches, taking as many as you can handle onto the needle before pulling it out and starting again. Following the pencilled line, continue sewing until you reach the other corner, or the end of the seam. Periodically check the reverse side of your sewing to see that your stitches are on the line there as well. Be careful not to stretch bias edges out of shape. When you reach the end of the line, take two tiny back stitches, one on top of the other, pull tight and clip your thread, leaving a tail of ½ inch for security (see illus. 24-a & c.)

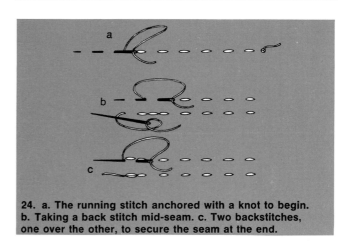

24. a. The running stitch anchored with a knot to begin. b. Taking a back stitch mid-seam. c. Two backstitches, one over the other, to secure the seam at the end.

Maintain firm tension on your sewing thread. Open the pieces you're sewing together and look at them from the front. Apply tension across the seam by pulling the fabric with your hands. If the seam pulls apart to show a ladder of stitches spreading between the pieces, you're handling your thread too loosely. Pull it up firmly, without drawing the fabric, of course.

When joining rows or segments, pin the crucial seams-that-must-match together without felling the seam allowances (see illus 25). When you sew longer seams, backstitch every 3 inches or so (see illus. 24-b), and backstitch when crossing previous seams without catching the seam allowances into the stitching. Stitch through the base of converging seam allowances to pinch them together at the seam point. Steam press when finished, fanning the seam allowances around points where they collect (see illus. 26).

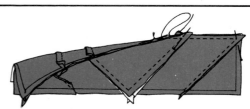

25. Handsewing two rows together, leaving seam allowances free.

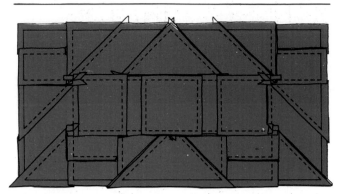

26. Hand pieced block with seam allowances pressed closer. Note the fanning of seam allowances around points where many seams converge.

Whether your needle is powered by hand or by machine, the three processes of piecing are the same: pin, sew, and press. The seam you sew should be straight and true, whether you're stitching ¼ inch inside an accurately cut straight-edge or following a pencilled line. When finished, your pieced block should lie flat and smooth with seam-lines running into each other and crossing exactly, outlining precise geometric areas of color. Overall, your block should measure the same in fabric as it does on paper, and every block thereafter should be identical. Beautiful!

Applique

For anyone who loves to sew a fine seam, applique is heaven. So many entrancing possibilities, all those colors, the variety of shapes to attach, each presenting its own little challenge to the fingers. Appliquers quickly develop their own formulas for getting fabric to do their bidding. They handle the material just so, they develop a fondness for one particular needle and a certain kind of thread, they combine a little of this method with a bit of that process. Applique is a sewing craft with many ways of reaching the finished goal: appliques with smooth, sharply defined contours securely attached to a background with stitching that serves the design without distracting from the total effect.

There's no right way to applique. There's only your way. The outlines that follow describe many of the procedures appliquers use to achieve the perfection they crave. My own personal method is explained in the instructions for Flowering Plum on page 111. Use whatever method or combination of methods strikes your fancy and eases the particular problems your project presents.

Applique is worked on the right side of the fabric. The outline on the front of each applique marks its finished shape. The seam allowance material between that pencilled outline and the cut edge of the applique must be hidden underneath the applique, giving it a folded, nonfrayable edge.

That reads simply enough. But in actuality fabric doesn't want to fold every which way into perfect curves, acute angles and spiky points. Getting that fold to follow the ins and outs of the pencilled line flawlessly is the major challenge of applique.

If you measure the pencilled outline and cut edge of an applique between any two points, they will differ unless both are straight lines. When the cut edge is smaller than the outline, as it is on inside curves and angles, the cut edge has to stretch before it can be turned under. When the cut edge is larger than the outline, as it is on outside curves and angles, the cut edge has to shrink to lie flat under the applique.

1. Clip the seam allowance around inside curves. Cut straight into the seam allowance at intervals, stopping three to five threads away from the pencilled outline. The deeper the curve, the closer the clips (see illus. 27-a).

2. Clip the seam allowance at inside angles. Center the cut between the sides of the angle, cutting right up to, but not across, the pencilled line (see illus. 27-b).

3. Clip or notch the seam allowance of outside curves. Make straight cuts or V cuts into the seam allowance at intervals, stopping three to five threads away from the pencilled outline. Use V notches on steep curves (see illus 27-c).

4. Fold the seam allowance across points. Creasing it level with the tip, turn the seam allowance above a point under the applique (see illus. 27-d).

5. Trim wide seam allowances. Trim seam allowances that are too wide or bulky to fit under the applique, leaving a scant 1/16 inch for the turn (see illus. 27-e). Seam allowances on convoluted shapes that curve in and out continuously can be trimmed to 1/16 inch to minimize the frequency of clipping.

Once you've arranged for the seam allowance to turn underneath the applique with the folded edge right on the pencilled outline, or just a smidgin inside the pencilled outline so that it will be concealed, you'll need to hold it there:

1. Basting: With single thread in a color that contrasts with the applique (easier to find when it's time to remove), sew the seam allowance in place (see illus. 28).

2. Pressing: Cut pressing templates from heavy paper or cardboard of file card weight. Center a template on the reverse side of the applique, fold the seam allowance over the edge of the template and iron it down. Remove the template to use on the next applique (see illus. 29). Pencilled outlines aren't necessary with this method, which is often combined with basting.

3. Lining: For every applique, cut a lining of press-on interfacing without seam allowances. Center the lining over the back of the applique, fuse it to the fabric with an iron, fold the seam allowance over the edge of the lining and press and/or baste through all layers. Press-on inter-

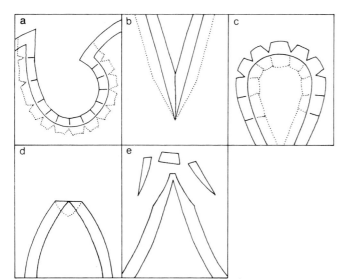

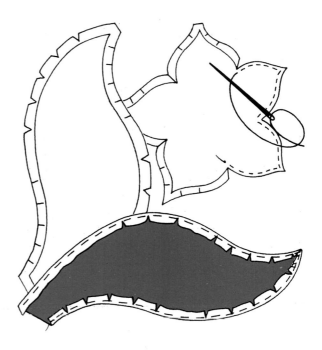

27. a. Clipping the seam allowance on an inside curve.
b. Clipping the seam allowance to the point of an angle.
c. Notching and clipping the seam allowance around
an outside curve. d. Folding back the seam allowance
above a point. e. Trimming the seam allowance above
and on either side of a narrow point. Dotted lines
indicate the seam allowance when turned underneath.

28. Appliques clipped and notched with seam
allowances basted down.

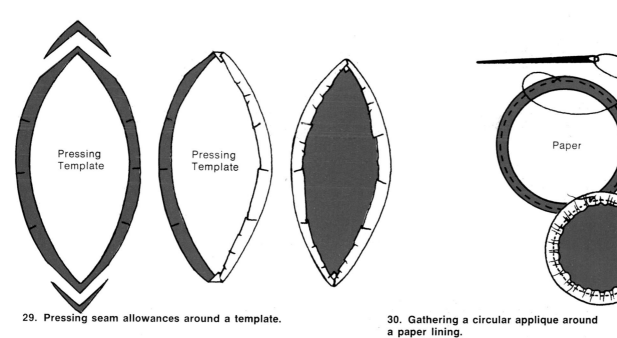

29. Pressing seam allowances around a template.

30. Gathering a circular applique around
a paper lining.

facing softens with use and washing but is stiff
in the meantime, which isn't a problem for non-
bed quilts. Round appliques can be gathered next
to the edge and pulled in around a heavy paper
lining, which is then removed (see illus. 30).
Pencilled outlines aren't necessary with these
methods.

4. Turn while sewing: Pinch-crease a fold into the
pencilled outline, turn the seam allowance under,
and stitch the applique to the backing immedi-

ately. Continue folding under just ahead of the
needle, shaping the applique as you sew. Stars
Over Hawaii and Christmas Star are appliqued in
the Hawaiian manner, a turn-while-sewing method but without any pencilled guidelines.

All of the applique designs in this book are
balanced and repeated. There's a plan behind the
position of every shape. To locate each applique
in its assigned place within an arrangement every
time you have to repeat the design, you can . . .

1. Trace: Make a full-size drawing of the block or unit you'll be repeating (see illus. 10-c on page 69). Or you can make a cardboard template of a design and trace around it.

2. Fold: Assuming that your background fabric is cut true and to size, fold it to make a succession of creases radiating from the center of a square or rectangle, or a succession of evenly spaced creases down the length of a strip. Use the creases to center your motifs (see illus. 31).

3. Measure: Following the grain of the fabric, measure and rule lines or make dots for positioning.

4. Judge by eye: Place all appliques on the background fabric and move them around until you find the right relationship.

Small appliques can be pinned in place on the background fabric, but large appliques may move off location during sewing causing the fabric behind the applique to twist and rumple — and that will change the size of the block or strip which, in turn, will cause problems when you assemble the quilt top. For prevention, particularly for beginners, baste appliques ⅛ inch from the edge to the background fabric. If an applique is large and delicate, baste down the center as well. Appliques should cover pencilled guidelines on the background fabric. You don't need to turn seam allowances underneath on the edges of appliques overlaid with another applique.

All of the appliques in this book are blindstitched, a kind of sewing that, when done correctly, is almost invisible:

1. Slip-stitched blindstitching: The applique is attached to the background fabric with stitches that run from inside the folded edge of the applique, through two or three threads of the background fabric, with the thread between tacks carried behind the farbic (see illus. 32).

2. Whip-stitched blindstitching: The applique is attached to the background fabric with tiny tacks that run over the edge of the applique into the background fabric, with the thread between tacks carried behind the fabric (see illus. 33).

Blindstitch with single thread in a color that blends into the applique. Unless colored threads from starts and stops are well hidden behind the applique, they can feather out beyond the edge and show through light background fabric. To anchor the applique securely, handle your thread with firmness. When whip-stitching in particular, stop after every four or five stitches and pull the thread taut; the tacks across the edge of the applique will all but disappear. After stitching, if you can lift the edge of the applique with your fingernail, your thread is either too loose or your stitches too widely spaced. Make your stitches a scant ¼ inch apart at the most, generally closer, and very dense around points and angles.

Use the tip of your needle to shove unruly seam allowances underneath, to smooth out any little points that mar a curved outline and, when seam allowances get down to almost nothing, to tease the threads of the fabric into a fold. Mary Borkowski switches to close buttonhole stitching to reinforce sharp points and angles. Mary also

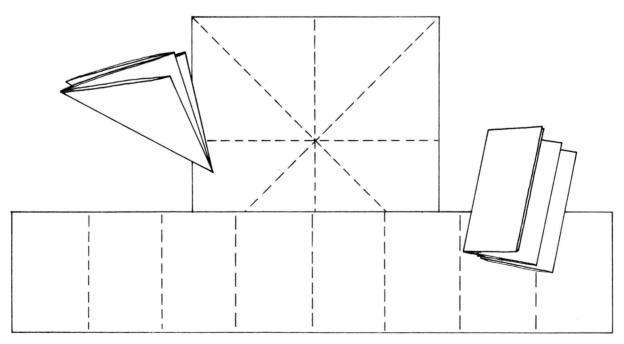

31. Making creases on background fabric to use for centering and spacing applique motifs.

pads her appliques occasionally, stopping ¼ inch or so before completing the stitching of an applique to push wisps of shredded batting or stuffing between the applique and the background fabric.

Narrow strips of fabric cut on the bias are used for curving lines and angles. If you're not using commercial bias tape, turn under and press the seam allowances on both long sides of the bias strips you cut, making bias tape as wide as the design requires. When stitching, thread two needles, one for each side of the tape. Stretching the tape slightly, blindstitch the outside of a curve first, then stitch the inside, easing the tape to fit the shorter length of the line. Stitch up to and slightly beyond the outside of an angle or corner first, then stitch with the other needle up to the turn. To miter the angle, stop and push the excess tape under the tape you've just attached, or divide the excess on either side of the miter like a pleat. After tacking the fold of the miter with a stitch or two, continue blindstitching (see illus. 34).

Use a hoop to embroider appliques after they have been stitched to the background. If you haven't already marked the embroidery design on the face of the applique, make an embroidery template, punching tiny holes through the lines of the design at intervals. Use the template to stencil dots on the applique indicating the path of the embroidery (see illus. 35).

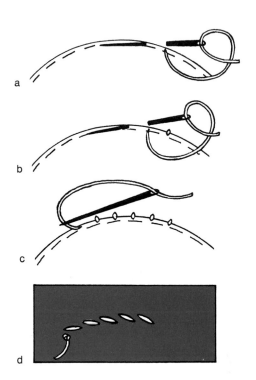

33. Whip-stitched blindstitching. a, b & c. Making the stitches. d. The stitching from the back.

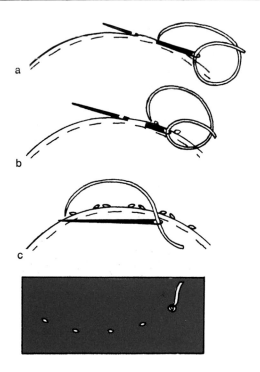

32. Slip-stitched blindstitching. a, b & c. Making the stitches. d. The stitching from the back.

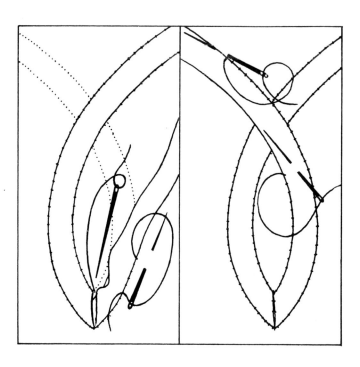

34. Appliqueing a bias strip and making a divided miter.

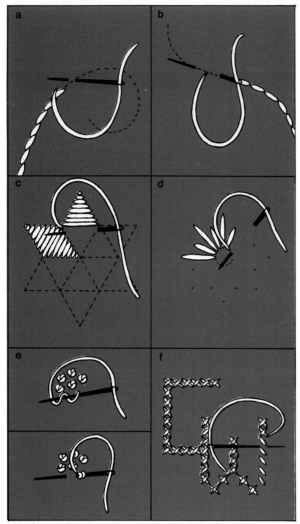

**35. Embroidery stitches: a. Stem stitch. b. Back stitch.
c. Satin stitch. d. Straight stitch. e. French knot.
f. Cross stitch.**

There's a controversy among quiltmakers about pressing applique. Some never press, feeling that the iron destroys the raised effect of the applique. The iron certainly destroys the raised effect of stuffed applique! Others, like myself, feel that pressing is the final finish, that quilting around the appliques provides all the "raising" needed. I place the block or section face down on a board with extra padding. After carefully aligning and straightening the sides of the fabric, returning it to the size and shape it was before applique began, I press with a damp cloth. To press or not to press — it's your choice, but I recommend pressing.

Assembling the top

This is where accuracy pays off. When you begin stitching all the parts together to make the top of your quilt, and each block and section matches the one next to it, putting your quilt together is a joy. You're not finished with old friend Accuracy yet, but the foundation you've prepared makes future collaboration easy.

The design of a quilt dictates how it will be constructed. Stars Over Hawaii and Vanishing Point are completely assembled when applique and piecing are finished. Peach Blossom is composed of panels. The other quilts in the book are structured more conventionally.

Assembling pieced blocks into a quilt top requires the same attention to matching seams that you lavished on the blocks themselves. Piece the blocks together in rows, pinning all crucial seams-that-must-meet together before you sew. Press those seams and then pin and sew the rows together. If you pieced by machine, pressing seam allowances of major seams open rather than closed may be necessary to reduce seam allowances clumping (see illus. 36).

Before you join the blocks for Queen's Petticoat, Starry Night or Sweet Dreams, you might enjoy experimenting with the setting arrangement. Lay the blocks out on the floor or a bed and face them in different directions to alternate and vary their relationship. The overall pattern and effect will change. You may like what you discover better than what you planned.

The blocks for Hawaiian Fruit Tree and Sunstar are separated by strips. Measure the side of one block. That measurement includes seam allowance, so cut strips that long and as wide as required. Sew the strips between the blocks that make up one row, and then assemble the other rows. Instead of trying to get an accurate measurement for a long row of floppy blocks with a tape measure, figure it out on paper, adding the finished size of every block to the finished width of each strip in the row. Cut and piece strips to sew between the rows accordingly, remembering to add a seam allowance at both ends of each strip. It also helps to measure and mark the reverse side of each strip with cross-lines to match with previous strips, assuring that the joint will form a perfect cross when stitched (see illus. 37). **Don't sew long strips between rows, or between blocks for that matter, without cutting to a measured size first.**

Appliqued quilt blocks are joined using piecing techniques. Blocks are stitched together in rows and the seams are pressed closed. After pinning to assure that seams between blocks will match in a neat +, the rows are joined to each other.

Figure border measurements on paper. Since borders are usually cut across the width of the fabric, they have to be pieced to make the distance. Center pieced seamlines when sewing borders around the quilt top. These seamlines are obvious, especially on solid fabric. When a quilt has many borders, like American Indian (page 56), the borders should be all butted or all mitered, not mixed (see illus. 38).

Butting is the easiest; stitch a border to each side, and then border the entire top and bottom. To miter a border you'll need to know the finished size your quilt top will be after that border is added. Cut and piece two borders to that length; cut and piece two borders to that width, adding seam allowances at the ends of each border. Match the center of each border to the center of the side, top or bottom to which it will be sewn; pin from that central point. Measure the loose border material at each corner; the measurements should match (adjust if they don't). Sew the borders around the quilt, stopping at each corner where the next seam begins. Ignoring the seam allowance, draw or fold a 45° angle from the point where two borders meet to the corner of the border. Fold one border over the other and blindstitch at the miter, or stitch together with right sides facing. Trim excess seam allowance (see illus. 39).

All of the quilts in this book are quilted in a frame or hoop. Queen's Petticoat can be worked that way or it can be constructed quilt-as-you-go with each block lap-quilted before the blocks are joined. The quilt-as-you-go method of building a quilt is explained in the instructions for Queen's Petticoat which begin on page 105.

Quilting: The Design

The directions for Stars Over Hawaii, Peach Blossom and Christmas Star specify marking quilting patterns on the fabric before basting the top to batting and lining. Peach Blossom and Christmas Star are marked before applique so the fabric must be marked with lines that will survive all that handling. Some quilters like to mark quilting patterns on blocks and strips when they are small, before seaming together into the quilt top. Others prefer marking when the quilt is stretched taut in frame or hoop. Unless there is a reason for marking at a particular stage, when you mark and how you mark are up to you. Read the instructions, study the quilting design, consider the options, make allowance for your quilting style and framing, and choose the easiest.

It is disconcerting, to say the least, to see a well-made quilt with good design and lovely colors spoiled by heavy pencil lines beside every quilted line on the pale background fabric! The quilting designs for Jackie's Tulips, Christmas Star, Peach Blossom, American Indian and Flowering Plum must be transferred to the cloth somehow — but that's not the way.

Pencils sharpened to a needle-point are favored by most quiltmakers for marking quilting patterns onto quilt tops. But pencils must be handled lightly to make a line that's barely visible before quilting, that will disappear into the shadow of the indentation after quilting. Soft lead writing pencils blur, smudge into adjacent areas and

soil quilting thread. A 2H or 3H artist's drawing pencil is my favorite; when marking fabric on a hard surface before basting with batting and lining, I often use a higher numbered pencil which makes dark lines impossible no matter how firmly I press. Mistakes can be removed with art gum, Windex diluted with water, or cleaning fluid.

On dark fabrics, I use colored pencils, pale blue, white, pink or yellow, purchased from an art supply store, which are soft-leaded but will still hold a point. Chalks have limited use for marking quilting patterns because they make such wide, blurry lines.

When **felt tip pens** that make water-erasable lines appeared on the market, quilters cheered! Lines that disappear when dabbed with water! They are magic, but they also have their peccadilloes. They need a quick, light touch or the fabric absorbs and spreads the ink like a blotter. Ironing may make the lines permanent and detergents may turn them brown. Test on scraps of fabric before using on your quilt top.

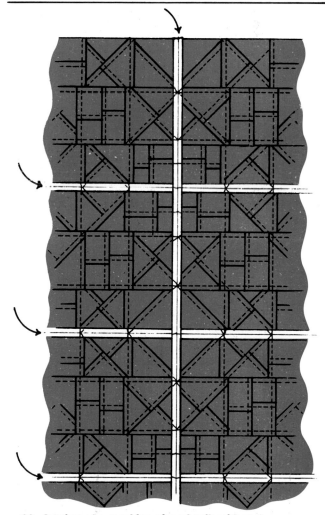

36. Section of a machine-pieced quilt with major seams pressed open to minimize clumping.

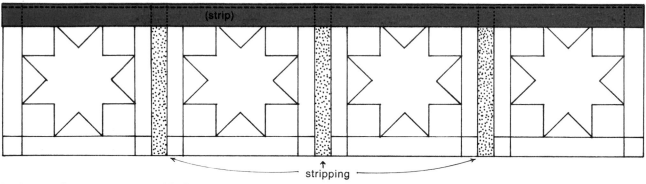

37. Long strip sewn to a row of blocks. Dotted lines marked on strip indicate match points.

stripping

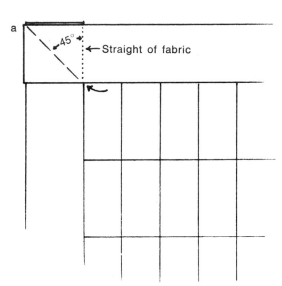

a

45°

←Straight of fabric

39. a. Folding to locate the seamline for a mitered corner. b. Blindstitching the miter.

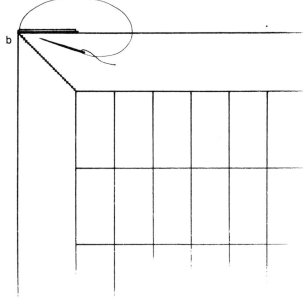

b

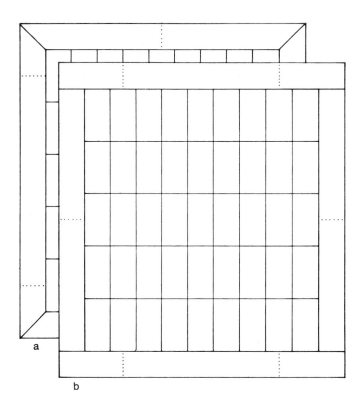

a

b

38. a. Border with mitered corners. b. Border with butted corners. Dotted lines indicate seamlines which are centered.

Slivers of very hard, left-over **soap,** shaved to an edge, make lines visible enough for quilting. Use white soap on dark fabrics; colored soap on light fabrics. For short lines, **needle-tracking,** scratching the fabric's surface with the point of a needle, makes a line that stays long enough for immediate quilting.

Some quilting patterns require no marking. Lines that are quilted ¼ inch from piecing seamlines or the edges of appliques, and that continue outward or inward a set distance apart, can be gauged by eye or finger. Quilting in the ditch needs no marking or gauging. But pictorial and decorative quilting patterns, patterns that fill the background with straight lines, and patterns composed of small forms need to be marked on the surface of the quilt, and marked repeatedly following a design plan.

Quilting patterns are traced outlines of the quilting design made on paper (see illus. 40-g). Fabric is pinned over the pattern, both are placed on a light box or window glass during daylight, and the design is traced onto the fabric. A pattern with sharp, dark lines may show through light background fabric sufficiently for tracing without light from behind. Paper quilting patterns are also used with dressmaker's carbon and tracing wheel, a method not recommended unless tested because tracing carbon dots are often obvious and permanent. Quilting patterns on Trace-A-Pattern, a material found in most full-service fabric stores, are pinned over the fabric; the lines of the design are followed with hard-pressed pencil; when the pattern is removed, the design is visible on the quilt top. Trace-A-Pattern material survives this treatment for eight to ten transfers.

Quilting templates are cut to shape with scissors or craft knife from stiff cardboard, transparent acetate, heavyweight Pellon® or other sturdy material. They are used for outline tracing on the fabric (see illus. 40-a, b, c & d). They're sometimes faced with sandpaper like cutting templates.

Quilting stencils, made from heavy paper, light cardboard, tracing paper, acetate, Mylar® or plastic, are perforated with holes or cut with slots along the quilting lines. After the design is traced on the stencil material, (1) lines are dotted with holes made by a sewing machine needle without thread (about six stitches per inch), or the design is hand punched with a large needle at crucial points (see illus. 40-b & e); or (2) the lines of the design are thickened and cut out, stencil-style, into long slots wide enough for a pencil point (see illus. 40-f). Perforated stencils are anchored to the quilt top and then pounded or rubbed with powdered cinnamon, paprika, flour, cornstarch, talcum or chalk which filters through the stencil holes leaving dots on the fabric. If your quilting technique is quick and feathery light, you can connect the dots with quilting before the powder disappears, but it's safer to connect the dots

with a line and then blow or brush the powder away. Perforated stencils can be used to dot the fabric with pencil marks which are then connected with a line. Lines are traced onto the fabric through the openings in slotted stencils.

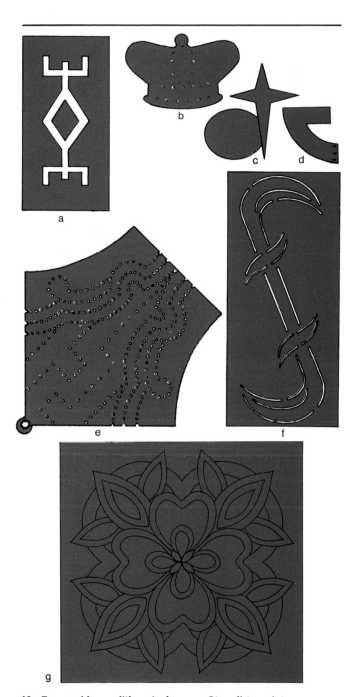

40. For marking quilting designs: a. Stencil template for American Indian. The diamond shape in the center is a separate template. b. Template for Christmas Star with holes indicating quilting lines. c. Simple templates for Along the River and Starry Night. d. Template for Oriental Blossom that is ¼ th of a design that reverses and repeats itself. e. Stencil for Starry Night with pivot hole strengthened by an eyelet. f. Slotted stencil for Symphony in F. g. Quilting pattern for Peach Blossom to be used for tracing.

Straight edges from rulers to long pieces of lumber to strips of cardboard, plastic, wood, acetate or paper are used to trace lines on a quilt top, and space the lines regularly. **Masking tape** can be stuck to the quilt's surface, quilted along one or both edges, and then removed and used again. And if you would like to improvise a circular design on your quilt top, **cups, saucers, plates, drinking glasses, compasses, spools** and **thimbles** can be pressed into service.

You're not bound by the quilting pattern used on the original of the quilt you're making. You can add your own touches or invent something in keeping with your conception and coloring of the quilt design. On quilts with patterns created by piecing or applique, quilting designs play a secondary role; they embellish, emphasize, blend, repeat, suggest and sometimes tell a story. Straight quilting lines in the background contrast and accent curving applique designs; areas quilted into a puckery texture dramatize unquilted shapes. Reviewing the different types of quilting (see illus. 41) may trigger an idea you can use to personalize your quilt.

Quilting: The Process

Frame or hoop? Each has its pros and cons. The quilting frame, which can expand or contract to present the entire width of a quilt with the extra length rolled onto stretchers, speeds the quilting of designs such as Hawaiian Fruit Tree and Vanishing Point with their long lines of quilting that travel from one edge of the quilt to the other. If you're involved with a group making one of our quilts to be raffled for the benefit of your Library's Acquisition Fund, you'll need a quilting frame to accommodate the number of workers quilting at the same time. But quilting frames take up space, which many of us don't have to spare these days. And when you're faced, from a stationary, frontal position, with quilting a design that winds around, in and out — you can imagine the contortions . . .

Quilting hoops are round or oval, the round hoop about 22 inches in diameter. You work on whatever section of the quilt is exposed within the rims of the hoop, which causes problems when your quilting design marches in straight lines across the face of the quilt. But if the design is pictorial, circular, or composed of little shapes that repeat, you can turn the hoop as the design turns to keep your needle moving comfortably toward you. Hoops are portable and take little storage space. But they do tend to work the quilt; it gets bundled, dragged and handled a lot during the time quilting requires. And the quilter is continuously swathed in quilt while quilting.

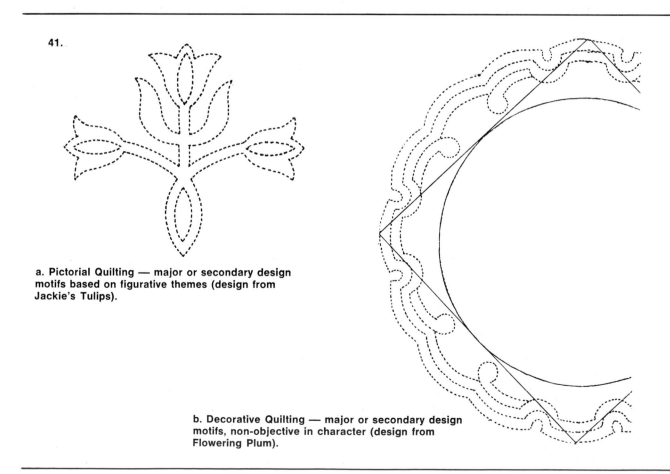

41.

a. Pictorial Quilting — major or secondary design motifs based on figurative themes (design from Jackie's Tulips).

b. Decorative Quilting — major or secondary design motifs, non-objective in character (design from Flowering Plum).

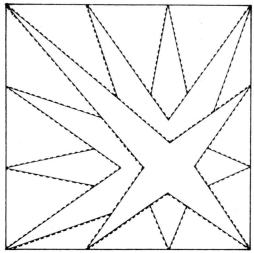

c. Quilting-in-the-ditch — accentuates pieced or appliqued shapes by quilting into the seamlines that outline the forms (example from Starry Night).

d. Outline Quilting — follows piecing seamlines at a set distance, usually ¼″ to ½″ (example from Evolution).

e. Contour Quilting — background quilting that repeats the outlines of appliqued shapes, moving outward concentrically (detail from Country Rose).

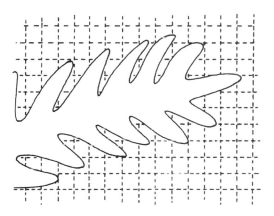

f. Background Quilting — grid and parallel line patterning, straight or curving, that fills non-design areas (section from Stars Over Hawaii).

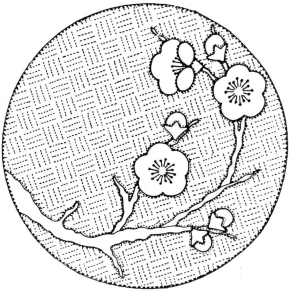

g. Texture Quilting — dense background patterning that contrasts with unquilted design motifs (example from Flowering Plum).

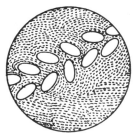

h. Stippled Quilting — solid background stitching (1/16″ or less) that makes adjacent unquilted areas stand out in relief (no example among quilts in book).

i. All-over Quilting — continuous lines that criss-cross the surface from edge to edge, uninterrupted by the fabric patterns they cross (no example among quilts in book).

The space you have available, the nature of the quilting your quilt requires, your mobility and personal preference will decide the question of frame or hoop for you. And you can always re-design the quilting pattern to suit the method.

If you're not using a sheet for lining, you'll be piecing it from yardage. When the lining you've chosen is a solid color, piece it so that the seam or seams are centered, but if the lining has a figure that will camouflage the seams, don't bother. And if you're going to quilt in a hoop, leave the excess lining to protect unfinished edges and hold the quilt in the hoop when quilting corners and edges. If your lining will also double as binding (see illus. **49** on page 94), **it** must be larger than the top. Even if you're quilting in a frame and will be binding with bias, add a safety measure of 4 inches to each dimension when making the lining. Seam allowances on linings are always pressed open.

Printed lining material distracts from quilting stitches, an advantage when they're not as nifty in back as they look in front. Stitches will blend into lining that is the same color as quilting thread, but the quilting design will still show nicely in relief. If your quilting stitches are marvels of regularity and your design a picture by itself, lining colored to contrast with quilting thread will show both off distinctly. Test whether lining color or print will shadow through and discolor the light fabrics in your quilt top. There will be a layer of batting in between, but it may not be enough to inhibit the situation.

Batting is available, packaged and folded, in standard sizes: 45 x 60 inches, 72 x 90 inches, 81 x 96 inches, 90 x 108 inches, and 120 x 120 inches. If purchased by the yard, 45 inches wide, it must be pieced by overlapping the edges about ½ inch and zigzag stitching the lengths together.

Polyester batting revolutionized quiltmaking and, more than any other factor, may be responsible for the Great Quilting Boom of the last fifteen years. Suddenly it wasn't necessary to crisscross the quilt with a network of stitches! Beginning quiltmakers could make a quilt leaving 8 inches — and sometimes more — between seams! Polyester is extremely resilient, washable, lightweight, non-allergenic and resistant to moths and mildew. But in the beginning it had one major disadvantage: it tended to migrate through the fabric in the quilt, giving the surface an unwelcome "bearded" appearance, particularly if polyester fabric was involved. It had one minor disadvantage: it didn't drape and lend itself to tiny quilting stitches like old-fashioned cotton batting.

Manufacturers came to the rescue with **bonded batting** which has a glaze applied to both sides of the batt that controls migration, although there is still concern among quiltmakers that bearding will occur in fabrics containing more polyester than cotton. **Needlepunched batting** is more blanket-like and soft than bonded batting, with less

loft, making it the desirable choice when delicate, decorative quilting is part of the design of the quilt.

Traditional cotton batting, although naturally absorbent, supple and thin enough for the finest quilting, pulls apart easily during handling and must be anchored by quilting at least every 2 inches to hold it together during washing. Even then it may mat and bunch. Recently, manufacturers have introduced an 80% cotton-20% polyester batt that they promise removes the disadvantages of both fibers — lack of stability in cotton and migration with polyester — while retaining the advantages of each.

Give your finished quilt top a final, thorough pressing. It's the last time it will ever feel an iron. Spread your lining, face down, on the floor or any other surface you can find where you can spread it out. Smooth it, straighten the grain lines, and tape the edges to the floor or carpet with masking tape every 12 inches so that it won't develop wrinkles when you can't see what's happening. Unfold the batting onto the lining without pulling or stretching, patting it smooth. Center the quilt top over the batting and lining. Keeping the layers smooth and unwrinkled, pin them all together every foot or so with straight pins or safety pins if you can use them only in seamlines where enlarged holes won't be seen.

With single thread in a long needle, baste the layers together, in radiating lines, working from the center to the edge. Working from the center out, cross those lines with a series of graduated squares or rectangles, ending with basting ½ inch inside the edges of the top (see illus. 42). Because they will be bunched and draped continuously while quilting is in progress, quilts prepared for quilting in a hoop must be basted closer than quilts to be quilted in a frame. For hoop quilting, fold extra lining material to the front and baste; it will keep batting from shredding and the edge of the quilt top clean.

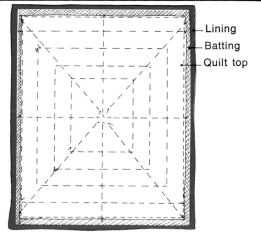

Lining
Batting
Quilt top

42. Top, batting and lining basted together in preparation for quilting.

To mount your quilt in the frame, begin by safety pinning or basting the top edge of the quilt to the fabric strip that covers one of the frame's stretchers. Roll most of the quilt up on that stretcher, then pin or baste the bottom edge of the quilt to the fabric strip that covers the other stretcher. Roll/unroll the quilt until the center portion is exposed and stretched firm between the two rolls.

If your quilting frame is narrow, you may not need to fasten the sides of the quilt to the sides of the stretcher frame. But if you want a taut quilt, or if your frame is wide to accommodate quilters on both sides, then safety pin a pair of muslin or twill tapes to the quilt at several points and tie them around the side bars of the frame. Or you can sew muslin strips to the sides of the frame and pin the edges of the quilt to them.

Quilters working at frames sometimes begin quilting at one end of the quilt and work toward the other end, but if you're quilting on a hoop, there's no choice: always begin quilting from the center and work outward to the edges. Place the center of your quilt over the inside rim of the hoop, push the outer rim down over both and tighten the wing nut on the screw while pulling the quilt taut and making sure that seam lines and fabric are straight. Use a table edge or chair back to support one end of the hoop while you're working.

Cut an 18-inch length of quilting thread (never longer — friction wears it thin), thread your needle and knot the end. Although not essential, waxing the thread with beeswax strengthens it and smooths its progress. Insert the needle into the top about ½ inch from where you want to begin, bringing it out on target. Tug gently until the knot pops through the fabric to lodge and

disappear forever within the batting (see illus. 43). If it should pop all the way out, or be too big to pull through the fabric, make another knot.

With the hand that isn't holding the needle underneath the quilt, palm up, insert the needle straight down through all the quilt's layers until you can feel it with the tip of the index finger beneath. Then move the point of the needle back up through the layers of the quilt to emerge on top (see illus. 44).

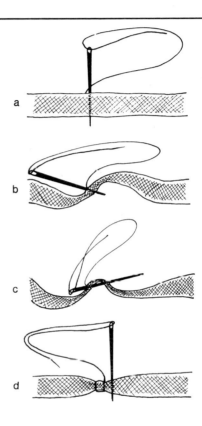

44. The quilting stitch.

That's the basic quilting stitch, one stitch after the other accumulating into a running stitch, which is what the American quilting stitch is called. It takes practice to perfect, and often a little bloodletting at the onset (dab with cold water to remove). Quilters use various devices to protect the index finger underneath — an oval of adhesive tape, a leather finger protector, little metal shields — but die-hard quilters insist that a needle prick is essential to stitch control. They recognize each other by the thickness of their finger calluses!

The goal is tiny, even stitches, fourteen to the inch says Mary Borkowski, our champion quilter. If you can achieve eight to ten stitches to the inch, counted on top only, you're doing very well. But it is more important for your stitches to be

a

b

c

⟵ Top
⟵ Batting
⟵ Lining

(Cross-section)

43. a. Beginning a quilting seam. b. Tugging the thread. c. Knot pulled into the batting.

regular, all the same size front and back, than it is for you to strain for a high count. Fabric weight and batting type and thickness will also affect the size of your stitches.

Every quilter develops a personal technique for manipulating the quilt to get that needle back up through all layers as quickly and as straight as possible. I create a ridge for each stitch by pressing down behind and in front of the needle while pressing up underneath the stitch. Some quilters wear a second flat-topped metal thimble on the forefinger of the hand underneath the quilt, letting the needle glance off the ridge of the thimble which also makes a ridge under the stitch, before deflecting back into the quilt. If you try to work the needle back into the quilt too quickly, catching only two or three threads of the lining in the stitch, that stitch will very likely pull out to leave a hole in the lining. Check your stitching from the lining side occasionally. And experiment with the tautness-slackness of the stretch of your quilt. If your quilt is pulled too tight, the needle is forced to return to the surface from an almost level position, enlarging the space between the stitches.

To start, concentrate on making one stitch at a time. Then try taking two or three stitches on your needle before drawing it out. If that's not comfortable, stick with one stitch at a time. When you cross a seam allowance you may have to stab stitch to retain even spacing. Insert the needle straight down and bring it out. With the hand underneath the quilt, reinsert the needle straight up and bring it out on top (see illus. 45). If you're ambidexterous, you can use this stitching technique exclusively, although the stitches on the back of your quilt won't be as even. For Christmas Star and Jackie's Tulips, Mary Borkowski quilts with a backstitch (see illus. 35 on page 84), using colored thread to bring quilting lines to the foreground.

When seam allowances are pressed to one side, you can quilt in the ditch over the seam, sewing on the side of the seam without seam allowances (see illus. 46) and changing sides when seam allowances reverse. Seams pressed open don't leave a ditch to quilt in. When outline quilting a pieced top, stay ¼ inch from the seam to avoid stitching through seam allowances (see illus. 47).

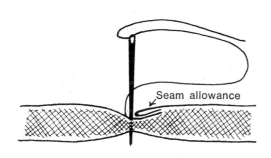

46. Quilting in the ditch.

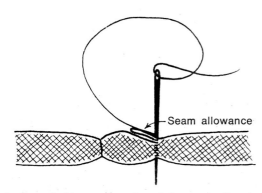

47. Outline stitching at the edge of the seam allowance.

When your needle gets sticky, as it will, run it through an emery bag several times. Scoot your needle through the batting to move from one line to another nearby. If you're quilting at a frame and the line makes a turn that's uncomfortable for you to stitch, stop and approach from another direction. Some quilters keep several needles in the quilt working different sides of a motif. When you get to the corners and edges of a quilt stitched in a hoop, you may want to extend the quilt with strips of muslin to have something for the hoop to grip.

Quilters disagree on The Right Way to secure a quilting seam. I feel safe taking a tiny backstitch, piercing the thread of the backstitch with my needle, moving the needle through the top into the batting, guiding it through the batting as far as it will reach before bringing it out on top where I clip the thread (see illus. 48). The long tail of the thread floats within the batting and it

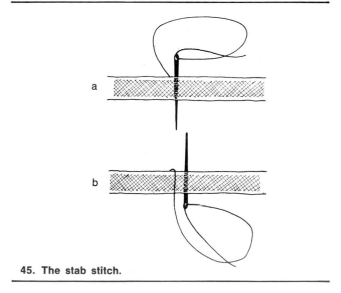

45. The stab stitch.

allows the quilting seam leeway to give under pressure without pulling out at the end. I leave tails on the thread at the beginning for the same purpose, hooking any bits that remain on the surface into the batting with the swipe of another needle.

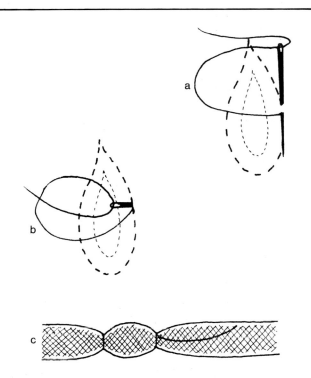

48. a. Securing a quilted seam with tiny backstitch.
b. Piercing the backstitch with the needle, running the needle through the batting before bringing it out on top.
c. After close clipping, the thread disappears into the batting.

Starts and stops that show are the absolute no-no-no of quilting. Someone inspecting your quilting should never be able to discover where you began and ended a thread. I hide telltale backstitches under the overhang of a seam when I can but, personally, I'd rather feel secure that my quilting won't come out than satisfy a persnickety judge.

Quilting is a rhythmic activity, quiet and soothing. It's therapeutic, like meditation to some. They cherish the time spent at hoop or frame, moving the needle in and out at a measured pace, building tiny stitches into lovely designs. It's satisfying, renewing and — fair warning! — it is addictive.

Binding the Edge

Take all the basting stitches out of your quilt and trim it evenly around the edge — unless you plan to use lining material or border fabric from the top as binding. In that case you'll need an extra ½ inch at least for the most narrow bound edge.

¼ inch (seen from the front) is the smallest finished binding possible on a quilt. For a ¼-inch binding of lining material, trim the batting even with the top; trim the lining even with top and batting plus ½ inch (¼ inch included for seam allowance). If your binding will be wider than ¼ inch, cut the batting wider to fill the binding. Turning the seam allowance under as you go, fold the lining-binding to the front and pin, then blindstitch to the top. Miter the corners. A final row of quilting in the ditch around the binding gives a firm, tailored feel to the edge (see illus. 49).

For a binding of border fabric from the top, the procedure is the same, only reversed. Since the binding on a quilt is usually the first to wear out, fold any extra material inside to double the binding.

The binding most frequently used on the quilts in the book is the narrow bias bound edge. Commercial bias binding can be purchased in standard colors, but for better quality, color choice and variety of width, make your own, and make it double for survival's sake. The formula for doubled binding is 2 x (binding width in front) x 2 + ½ inch. Determine how much binding you'll need to go around the four sides of the quilt. For a ½-inch binding, I usually add about 12 inches to allow for mitering the corners.

Bias stripping can be simply and efficiently made from a square of fabric, cut diagonally from corner to corner, with the resulting triangles seamed together into a rhomboid. Stitch the straight-of-fabric edges (not the bias edges) together to make a tube with one side of the seam overhanging the other by the depth of the binding. After the seams are pressed open, begin cutting at the overhang, measuring with a ruler ahead of the scissors, until the entire tube is a pile of continuous binding (see illus. 50).

Fold and press the binding in half lengthwise, with right sides outside. Matching the two cut edges of the binding to the cut edge of the quilt top, stitch binding to each side of the quilt through all layers (preferably by machine), stopping where seam meets seam at each corner. At each corner allow extra material for the miter. After mitering each corner, turn the binding to the back of the quilt. Blindstitch the folded edge of the binding to the lining, covering the seam (see illus. 51).

Binding can be as wide as you want to make it. It can be so wide that it looks more like a border than a simple binding. However wide it is, binding should feel as full of batting to its edge as the quilt itself. Insert extra batting if necessary. I sometimes roll surplus batting into the binding, making an edge that's rounded like soft, fat cording. And when binding a quilt with four straight sides, I use straight rather than bias binding. Bias binding is required for turning the rounded corners of quilts such as Peach Blossom and Flowering Plum.

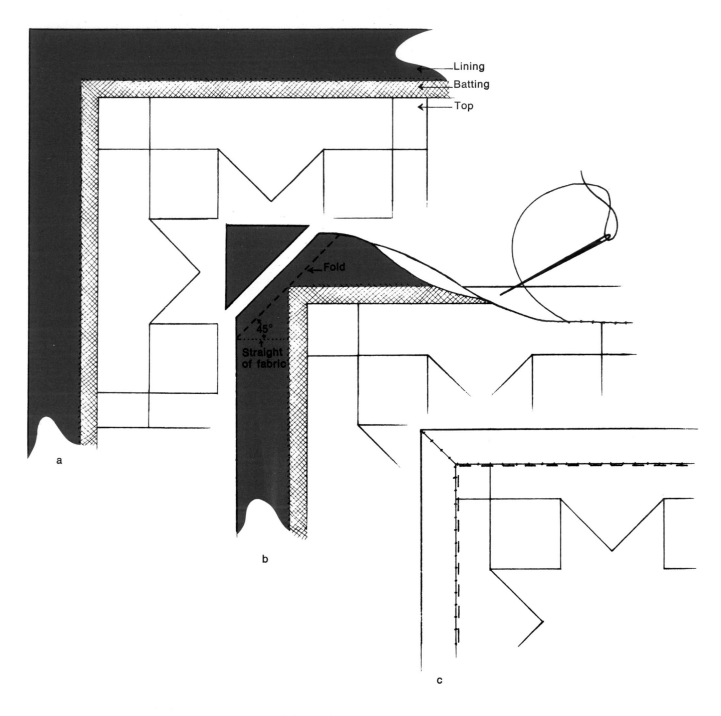

Lining
Batting
Top
Fold
45°
Straight
of fabric

a

b

c

**49. a. Preparation for binding with the lining.
b. Stitching in progress and corner trimmed for mitering.
c. Finished miter with binding seam quilted in-the-ditch.**

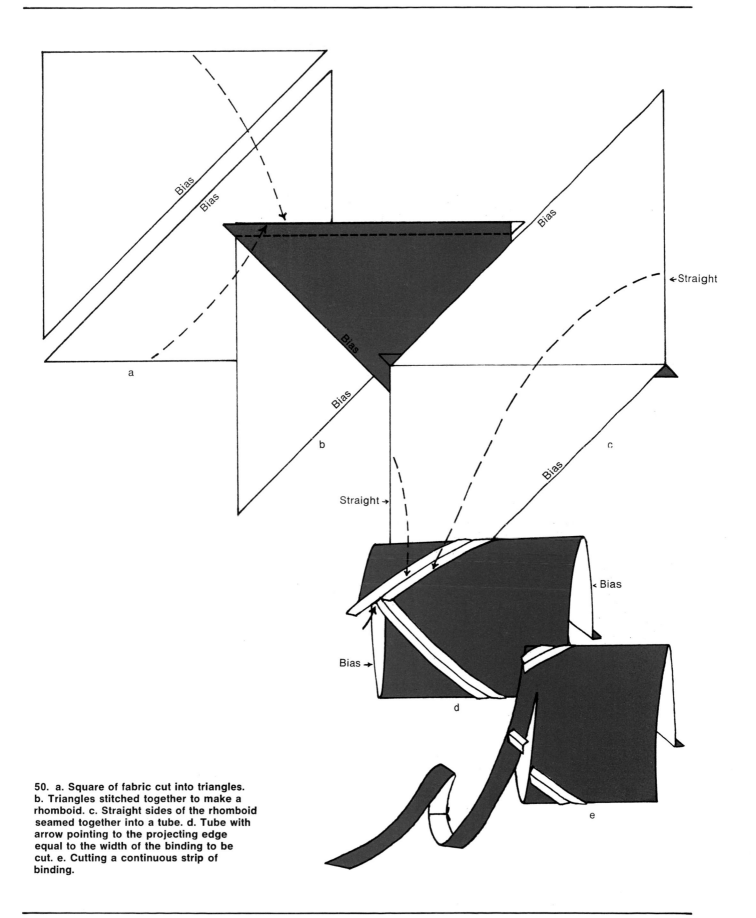

50. a. Square of fabric cut into triangles. **b.** Triangles stitched together to make a rhomboid. **c.** Straight sides of the rhomboid seamed together into a tube. **d.** Tube with arrow pointing to the projecting edge equal to the width of the binding to be cut. **e.** Cutting a continuous strip of binding.

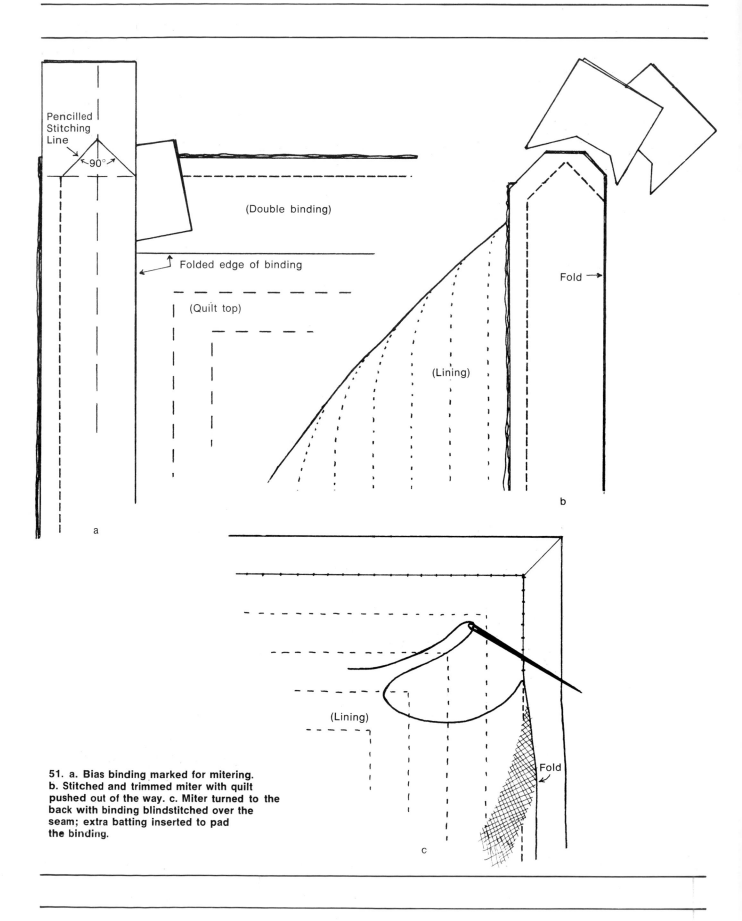

Pencilled
Stitching
Line

90°

(Double binding)

↑ Folded edge of binding

(Quilt top)

a

Fold →

(Lining)

b

(Lining)

Fold

c

51. a. Bias binding marked for mitering.
b. Stitched and trimmed miter with quilt
pushed out of the way. c. Miter turned to the
back with binding blindstitched over the
seam; extra batting inserted to pad
the binding.

An alternative to the bias bound edge, the hemmed edge, would be an effective finish for Peach Blossom or Flowering Plum. After trimming the edges of batting and lining to match the top, cut the batting back an additional ¼ inch. Turn ¼-inch seam allowance on the top and lining inside and blindstitch the folded edges together over the batting. You'll need to stop all quilting at least ½ inch from the edge or you won't be able to turn the seam allowance inside. Extra rows of quilting can be added when the hemming is finished (see illus. 52).

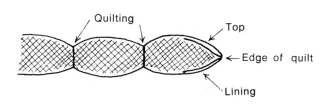

52. Side view of a quilt with a hemmed edge.

The Signature

The last is the best. Sign your quilt. At the very least, sign it with your initials and the date. At the most, you can include a complete dedication, a favorite poem, the history of the quilt from how long it took to make to who helped and what happened along the way. Posterity will be grateful.

The usual place for a signature is in back at one corner of the lower edge. The worst place for a signature is in front in large contrasting colored lettering that blatantly destroys the harmony of the design. There's no reason you should not sign in front, I often do, especially if the quilt is to be hung, but I choose a spot that is unobtrusive, solidly colored, and I use embroidery floss that matches. A signature can also be quilted. Either way, the information is there but it doesn't shout.

A signature embroidered into the top or lining, rather than embroidered on a label which is stitched to the quilt, can never be separated from the quilt as long as it is in one piece. Use your own handwriting or print neatly and then backstitch or stem stitch over the lines. Or cross stitch your initials and the date (see illus. 35 on page 84).

If you want to say more than you have the patience to embroider, write it on a light colored piece of fabric with indelible felt-tip pen or a liquid embroidery marker. Wash and iron the piece to be sure the writing is permanent and won't fade. Blindstitch it neatly to the quilt in back or better yet, piece it into the lining before you baste the quilt sandwich together, and quilt it into the structure.

Display and Care

To hang your quilt so that its weight will be distributed over every inch of the top edge, so that it will fall straight and be easy to take down: From a lumberyard, get a piece of stripping about ¼ inch to ½ inch thick and 2 inches wide, as long as the top of your quilt less an inch if you don't want it to show. Prepare to mount the strip on a wall for one of these two methods: (1) Tack a strip of Velcro® to the wood and stitch the other half of the Velcro® to a strip of muslin. Baste the muslin across the top edge of the quilt in back. (2) Cut a strip of muslin 6 to 8 inches wide and as long as the strip of wood. Sew the long sides of the muslin together to make a tube, or sleeve. Baste the sleeve across the top edge of the quilt in back. Insert the piece of wood, or a metal rod, into the sleeve.

If your quilt has to live in a closet for a while, store it wrapped in cloth; an old sheet is perfect. Never use plastic — a quilt needs to breathe. Take it out occasionally and fold it differently so that creases won't become a permanent part of the surface.

If you used polyester batting, washed all fabrics together before beginning to cut, and stitched securely, you should have no qualms about laundering your quilt when it gets dirty. More damage is done to fabrics by allowing dirt and grime to remain in the material for fear of water than by the water itself. Use warm water, mild detergent or soap, a gentle cycle and give it an extra rinse. Dry it flat, spread over an old sheet on the lawn in the shade or on the floor. Or hang it supported by two lines. A wet quilt is too heavy to hang from one end only.

Instructions & Patterns

STARRY NIGHT
Shown on page 15

Materials: 45-inch cotton or cotton/polyester blend fabric in the following colors and amounts: 2 yards of white, ¼ yard light blue print, ¼ yard dark blue print, 1¼ yards dark blue, ¾ yard light purple print, ½ yard dark purple print, 1½ yards purple plus 3 yards purple for border, 1 yard light burgundy print, 1 yard dark burgundy print, 2½ yards burgundy plus 3 yards burgundy for border, 4¾ yards burgundy for lining, ¾ yard light red print, ½ yard dark red print, 2 yards red; needle and quilting thread in white and burgundy, polyester batting, sewing machine, ruler, pencil, paper, white glue, cardboard, craft knife.

Quilt is 92 x 100 inches.

To make working patterns (templates): Using a ruler to guide your pencil, draw an exact copy of each pattern piece on sturdy cardboard. Cut each cardboard pattern piece out with a craft knife held against the edge of a ruler.

Cutting the pattern pieces for the blocks: Refer to the cutting chart for the number of pattern pieces you'll need to cut from each of the various fabrics. Star pattern pieces are designated with numbers (1 thru 6); background pattern pieces are marked with letters (A thru D).

45″ FABRIC		CUT	
			Pattern Pieces
FORE-GROUND STARS	Fabric #1 — 2 yds.	1	56
	WHITE	2	128
CENTRAL UNIT	Fabric #2 — ¼ yd.	3	8*
	LIGHT BLUE PRINT	4	8*
	Fabric #3 — ¼ yd.	5	16*
	DARK BLUE PRINT	6	16*
	Fabric #4 — 1¼ yds.	A	48
		B	16
	DARK BLUE	C	16
		D	8
INNER BORDER	Fabric #5 — ¾ yd.	3	24*
	LIGHT PURPLE PRINT	4	24*
	Fabric #6 — ½ yd.	5	48*
	DARK PURPLE PRINT	6	48*
	Fabric #7 — 1½ yds.	A	64
		B	32
	PURPLE	C	48
		D	24

45″ FABRIC		CUT	
			Pattern Pieces
MIDDLE BORDER	Fabric #8 — 1 yd.	3	40*
	LIGHT BURGUNDY PRINT	4	40*
	Fabric #9 — 1 yd.	5	80*
	DARK BURGUNDY PRINT	6	80*
	Fabric #10 — 2½ yds.	A	32
		B	24
	BURGUNDY	C	80
		D	40
OUTSIDE BORDER	Fabric #11 — ¾ yd.	3	16*
	LIGHT RED PRINT	4	40*
	Fabric #12 — ½ yd.	5	24*
	DARK RED PRINT	6	56*
	Fabric #13 — 2 yds.	A	24
		B	16
	RED	C	56
		D	40

*When using fabrics with a right and wrong side, such as the prints used in the "Starry Night" quilt, reverse the pattern when cutting half of the fabric pattern pieces.

To cut each piece: Aligning arrows with the straight of the material, place template on fabric. With a sharp pencil, trace around template; cut out on the traced line. Because accurate, easy machine piecing depends on precise cutting, check each fabric pattern piece against the template to be sure it is an exact duplicate of the template's shape.

Arrange the fabric pieces for one block, right side down, in position as they will be sewn. See illustration A.

Check the illustration to be sure that background colors are correct and in the proper place. With right sides facing, align the cut edges of the two pieces to be stitched together. Sew an even ¼ inch inside the cut edge, setting the stitch regulator on your machine to make very small, tight stitches. Start each seam at its inner corner, moving toward the edge that will be on the outside of the block. Be careful not to stretch bias edges when stitching and pressing. After every step, replace the stitched unit in its place in your block arrangement so you'll always know "where you are."

Piecing sequence for each block (36 blocks):
First, join 5 and A (four pairs), join 6 and C (four pairs), join 4 and D (two pairs), join 3 and B (two pairs). Press seam allowances closed over the background pieces. See illustration B.

Next, join 5-A and 2 (four seams), join 6-C and 3-B (two seams), join 3-B and 2 (two seams), join 6-C and 4-D (two seams), join 4-D and 1 (two seams). Press seam allowances closed in the direction of the background pieces. See

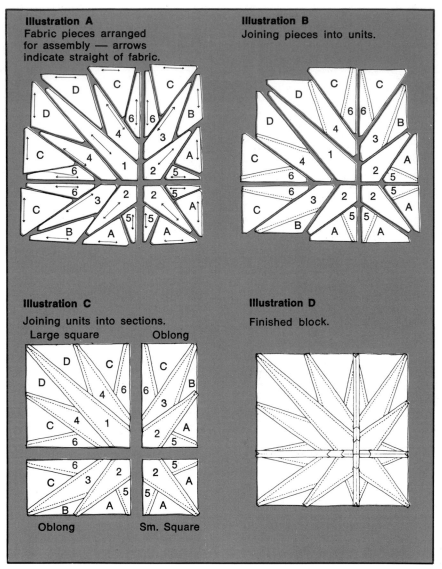

Illustration A
Fabric pieces arranged for assembly — arrows indicate straight of fabric.

Illustration B
Joining pieces into units.

Illustration C
Joining units into sections.
Large square   Oblong

Oblong   Sm. Square

Illustration D
Finished block.

illustration C.
Next, join large square and oblong, join oblong and small square, join 2 sides. Press seam allowances open and damp press the block. See illustration D.

After completing the 36 blocks that make up the main body of the quilt, make up the 20 large squares, four small squares and 16 oblongs that are used to piece the outside border (refer to illustration C).

Arrange the finished blocks for the central unit, the inner border and the middle border into the setting illustrated (see quilting setting illustration). Stitch the blocks together in rows of six. Stitch the six rows together to form the central

area. To reduce clumping regulator on your machine to where seam allowances converge, press seam allowances open.

Cut strips of purple fabric 2½ inches wide. Piece together to make a strip long enough to border the pieced "Starry Night" blocks (about 10 yards). With right sides together, sew purple border strip to each side and then across top and bottom of pieced blocks (¼-**inch seam allowance); miter** each corner.

Cut strips of burgundy·fabric 4½ inches wide for outer border. Piece together to make a strip long enough to surround quilt top (about 11 yards). With right sides together, sew to each side and then across top and bottom of quilt (¼-inch **seam allowance**); miter each corner.

To make lining you will need 4¾ yards of 45-inch fabric, cut in half and seamed together or 7 yards of 36-inch wide fabric, cut in thirds and seamed together. Baste lining, batting and quilt top together for quilting in a hoop or frame. Lining should be ¾ inch larger all around to be turned to top of quilt for binding after quilting is completed.

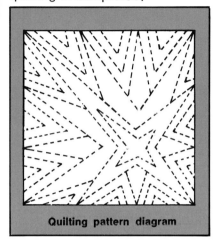
Quilting pattern diagram

To quilt, outline points of star shapes by quilting in the ditch only where seam allowances have been pressed closed. Quilt a mini-star inside each foreground star and add outline quilting lines ¾ inch apart inside the background areas. Use white thread for quilting on white fabric and burgundy thread on all other colors.

To quilt border: Use mini-star design used in center of white stars on main body of quilt. Space these stars out as follows: one in each corner of border with long point to corner of pieced portion of quilt; one star at each side of this corner star angled so that long points of all three stars meet at corner of pieced portion of quilt. Stars on either side of each corner three-star motif point the other way with side points meeting side points of previously quilted star. Next stars change direction so that long points meet long points

of previously quilted stars. Continue quilting stars, reversing direction of adjacent stars, working from corners to center of each side. Adjust spacing and angle of stars so that stars in center of each side will meet properly.

In the larger space between every two stars, quilt a diamond shape. In the large W-shaped space between the long points of every two stars (in the purple inner border), quilt a smaller W-shape, following the star outlines.

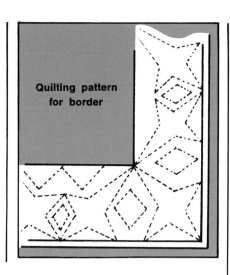
Quilting pattern for border

Quilt Setting Diagram

Center of quilt

When quilting is completed, turn excess background fabric to front of quilt. Folding edge of background fabric under, blindstitch to top of quilt, making a narrow binding all **around. Miter corners.** Finish with a row of quilting in the ditch at the inside edge of binding.

Starry Night Quilt Setting
Size of pieced blocks when joined — 80 x 88 inches.
Size of finished quilt — 92 x 100 inches.
Size of one "Starry Night" quilt block — 12 x 12 inches.

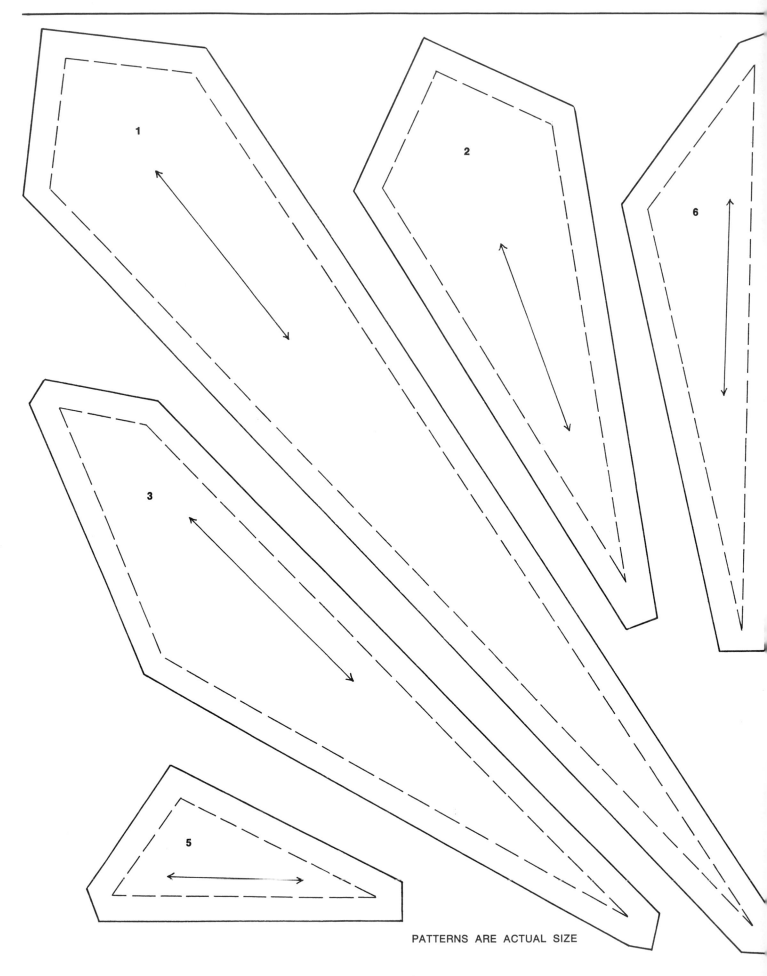

PATTERNS ARE ACTUAL SIZE

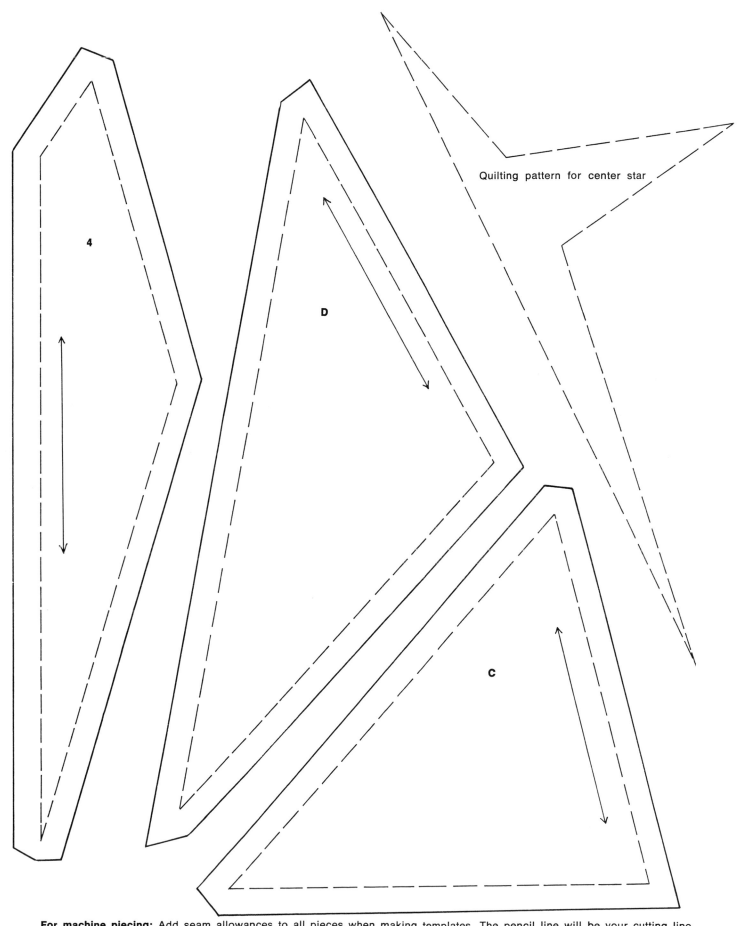

Quilting pattern for center star

4

D

C

For machine piecing: Add seam allowances to all pieces when making templates. The pencil line will be your cutting line.
For hand piecing: Do not add seam allowances to pieces when making templates. Add seam allowance when cutting fabric. The pencil line will be your sewing line.

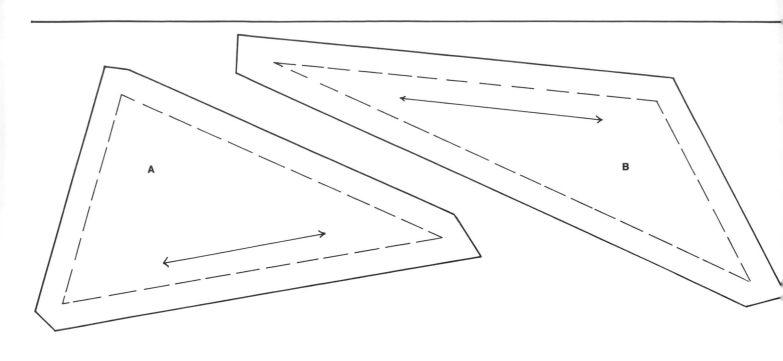

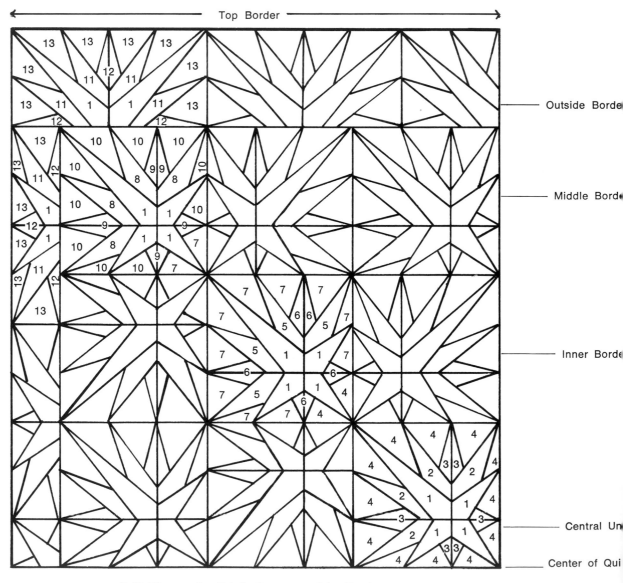

Quilt Diagram for Fabric Arrangement by Number.

QUEEN'S PETTICOAT WALL TAPESTRY or BED

Shown on page 17

Materials: Select a combination of cotton, polyester, rayon, silk, wool, etc. fabrics with colors and textures that complement and contrast. Use 100% cotton or cotton-polyester blends for a bed quilt (see chart).

You will also need bonded polyester quilt batting to size, sewing thread and quilting thread.

COLOR CODE FOR "QUEEN'S PETTICOAT" QUILT

"A"—Dark brown velvet; "B"—Dark brown print with turquoise, cotton; "C"—Light brown cotton print; "D"—Off-white cotton (muslin); "E"—Turquoise; "F"—Solid camel-color cotton; "G"—Stripe/print in camel, cotton; "H"—Gray cotton.

Cutting: Using the full-size patterns, cut templates from cardboard, plastic, metal, wood, or any other rigid, sturdy material. Placing a template on the wrong side of the fabric, trace its outline with a sharp pencil, marking a stitching line and/or cutting line for each piece. Precise, consistently accurate outlines are essential for accurate piecing and matching of shapes.

45-inch Fabric	For	Wall Tapestry 56 x 80 inches	Bed Quilt 80 x 92 inches
"A"	Piecing & Binding	1¾ yds.	2¾ yds.
"B"	Piecing	1 yd.	1¾ yds.
"C"	Piecing	¾ yd.	1 yd.
"D"	Piecing	¾ yd.	1¼ yds.
"E"	Piecing & Border	1½ yds.	3 yds.
"F"	Lining squares	1½ yds.	2½ yds.
"G"	Lining squares	1½ yds.	2½ yds.
"H"	Lining border	1 yd.	2¼ yds.

Cut: Fabric & Pattern	1 Block	Wall Tapestry (24 Blocks)	Bed Quilt (42 blocks)
A/B	4	96	168
B	2	48	84
B	4	96	168
C	6	144	252
A	2	48	84
A	2	48	84
D	6	144	252
E	4	96	168

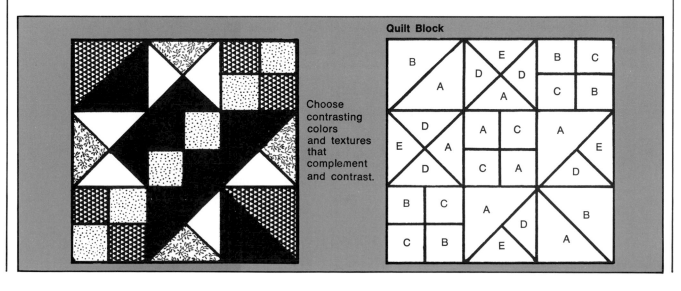

Choose contrasting colors and textures that complement and contrast.

Quilt Block

Stitching blocks: Blocks may be sewn by hand or by machine. Where seam-lines cross or meet, pin to match exactly before seaming. Press seam allowances closed after each step. Trim seam allowances that extend beyond ¼ inch. See chart at right.

Preparing blocks for quilting: (Amounts for bed quilt are given in double parentheses.) Cut 24 ((42)) squares of batting 12 x 12 inches. Cut 12 ((21)) squares of lining fabric "F" 12½ x 12½ inches. Cut 12 ((21)) squares of lining fabric "G" 12½ x 12½ inches. Place a quilt block face down on a flat surface. Center a square of batting over the wrong side of the quilt block. (**Note:** batting will not cover quilt block seam allowances). Cover both with a lining square matching lining edges with the edges of the block. Baste all three layers together around the outside and criss-cross from corner to corner. Repeat for all remaining blocks. See illustration.

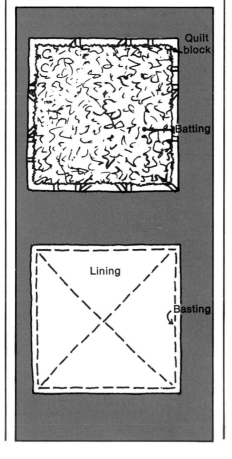

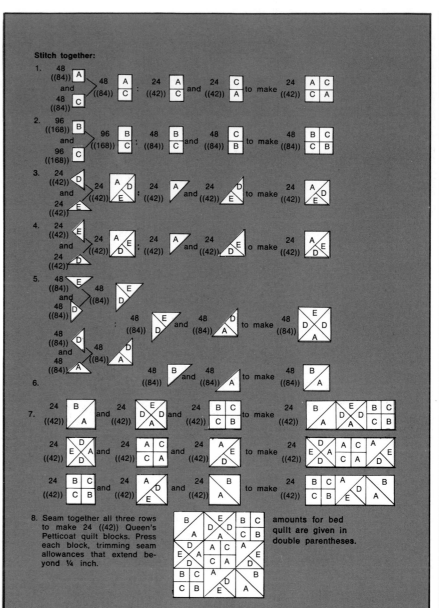

Initial quilting of each block: Using the patterns, make quilting templates from cardboard or heavyweight Pellon®. Major quilting lines are ¼ inch inside piecing seamlines, where seam allowances end. Quilting patterns cross seamlines where adjoining fabrics match. Trace around the appropriate quilting template with sharp colored pencil or chalks. Quilting guidelines should be barely visible before quilting, and invisible after quilting. See illustration.

NOTE: All quilting must stop at least ½ inch from the edges of the block.

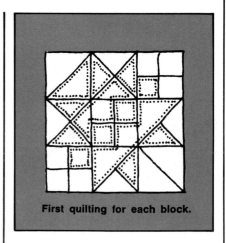

First quilting for each block.

Joining pre-quilted blocks: All blocks are first joined together in pairs, stitching an "F" lined block to a "G" lined block.

106

Remove basting threads. Fold and pin lining and batting layers back as far as quilting will allow to expose the edges of the pieced quilt blocks that will be stitched together. With right sides facing, seam the pieced blocks together, matching seamlines that cross.

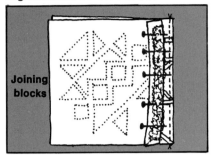

Open the blocks and place face down on a flat surface. Finger-press the seam allowance to one side. Unpin lining and batting. Smooth the batting down, trimming any overlap so that batting edges butt neatly over the seam. With large, loose stitches, overcast batting edges together. See illustration.

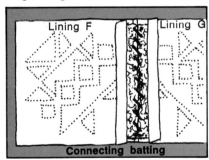

Connecting batting

Smooth lining down over the batting, one edge over the other. Turn under the top lining seam allowance (¼ inch); blindstitch the folded edge to the lining of the adjoining block, but don't stitch into the pieced blocks in front.

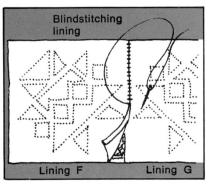

Blindstitching lining

Lining F   Lining G

Secondary quilting and block assembly: Turn joined quilt blocks face up and quilt over and next to the new seamline. Note the diamond motif quilted inside the newly-formed center square (quilting pattern A). See illustration.

Join the block pairs into squared units-of-four. As described previously, seam the

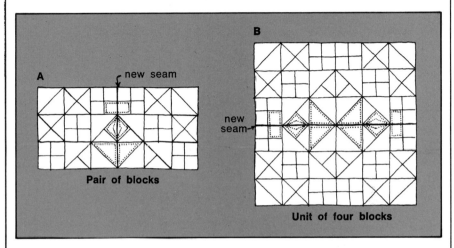

A
new seam
Pair of blocks

B
new seam →
Unit of four blocks

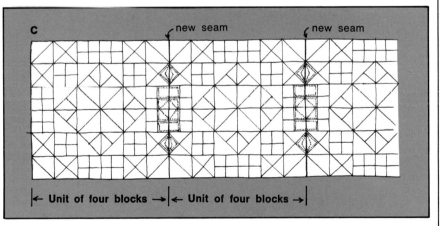

C
new seam   new seam

← Unit of four blocks →|← Unit of four blocks →|

pieced tops together, overcast adjoining batting edges, and blindstitch one lining edge over the other. For the wall tapestry, join all pairs into six units-of-four. When making a bed quilt, join enough pairs of blocks to make nine units-of-four, leaving three pairs as is. Turn the joined quilt blocks face up and quilt over and next to the new seamline. See illustration B. (**Note:** You may find it easier to use a hoop when quilting in the center of large units.)
Following the same procedures,

join three units-of-four together, making a cross-section of the quilt six blocks long and two blocks deep. In back, lining squares "F" should alternate with lining squares "G" checkerboard style. Turn face up and **quilt across the new seamlines.** Quilt a square-within-the-square where the blocks meet to form a new design element. See illustration C.

The wall tapestry is composed of two cross-sections. For the bed quilt, make one more cross-section and join the left-over pairs of blocks into a strip six blocks long and one block wide.

Join the cross-sections, matching seamlines when stitching the pieced block edges together, alternating linings "F" and "G". Add the strip of six blocks to the bed quilt. Quilt across the new seam, using a template to mark and quilt the star motif (quilting pattern B) inside the square formed where units meet. See illustration D.

Bordering, binding and final quilting: Cut and piece lengths of fabric "E" and "H" to border the quilted blocks in front and in back:

To prepare mitered corners: Fold both ends of each border strip to get a 45° angle, crease, cut on the crease, and pencil a stitching line ¼ inch inside the cut edge. See illustration.

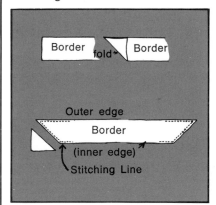

Along one side of the quilted blocks, fold back and pin the lining and batting layers as far as the quilting will allow, exposing the reverse side of the pieced blocks. With right sides facing, pin-baste and then stitch (¼ inch seam allowance) a border strip "E" to the pieced blocks, maintaining an even tension on both fabric edges. (Duplicate any changes in border length on all other same-size strips.) On the same side of the quilted blocks, fold back and pin the bordered-and-pieced top and batting layers, exposing the lining's reverse side. With right sides facing, pin-baste and then stitch a border strip "H" to the lining. Repeat, sewing borders to all sides of the quilted blocks. With right sides facing, **stitch the mitered corners.**

Cut 5 inch strips of batting to insert between the top and lining borders. Butt the edges of the border batting to the edges of the batting inside the blocks and whip them together. Smooth the borders over the batting. Baste all three layers

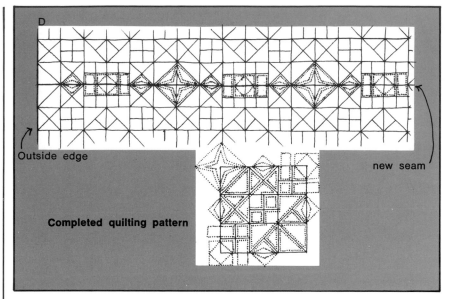

Completed quilting pattern

	Fabric "E" (top)	Fabric "H" (lining)
Wall Tapestry	2 strips 81 x 4½ inches 2 strips 57 x 4½ inches	2 strips 81 x 4½ inches 2 strips 57 x 4½ inches
Bed Quilt	2 strips 81 x 4½ inches 2 strips 93 x 4½ inches	2 strips 81 x 4½ inches 2 strips 93 x 4½ inches

together around the outside, matching top and lining border edges.

The batting will project about ¾ inch beyond the border fabric. Add another row of basting around the middle of the border.

Cut enough strips 1½ inches wide from fabric "A" to piece together approximately 302 inches of binding for the wall tapestry and 354 inches for the bed quilt. Bind the outside edges of the border, stitching through all layers, folding excess batting inside the binding. The binding seam allowance is ¼ inch; the finished binding is ½ inch wide.

Complete the quilting of the

outside of the pieced blocks, extending the quilting into the border as illustrated. Quilt the border, outlining ¼ inch inside its inner and outer seamlines, using a quilting template to mark and quilt the repeating diamond design (quilting pattern C). Remove basting threads. See illustration.

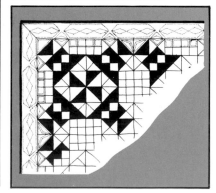

PATTERNS ARE ACTUAL SIZE

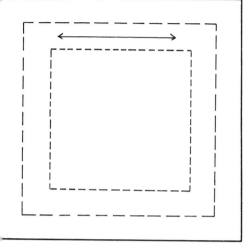

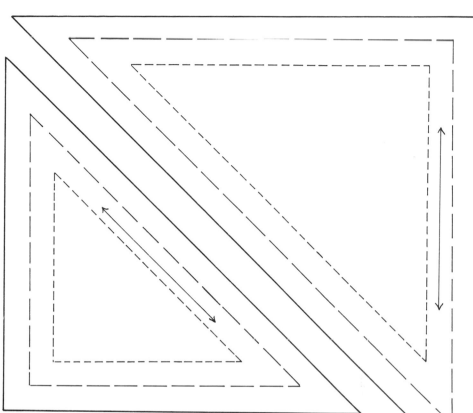

Photograph Showing Back of Queen's Petticoat

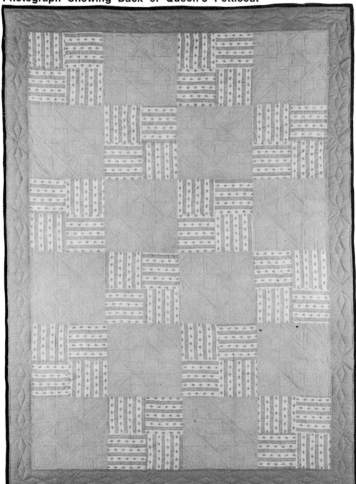

For machine piecing: Add seam allowances to all pieces when making templates. The pencil line will be your cutting line. **For hand piecing:** Do not add seam allowances to pieces when making templates. Add seam allowance when cutting fabric. The pencil line will be your sewing line.

Quilting Pattern A

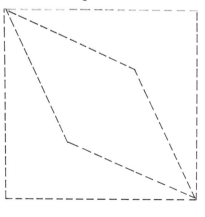

——— Cutting line

— — — Sewing line

- - - - - Quilting line

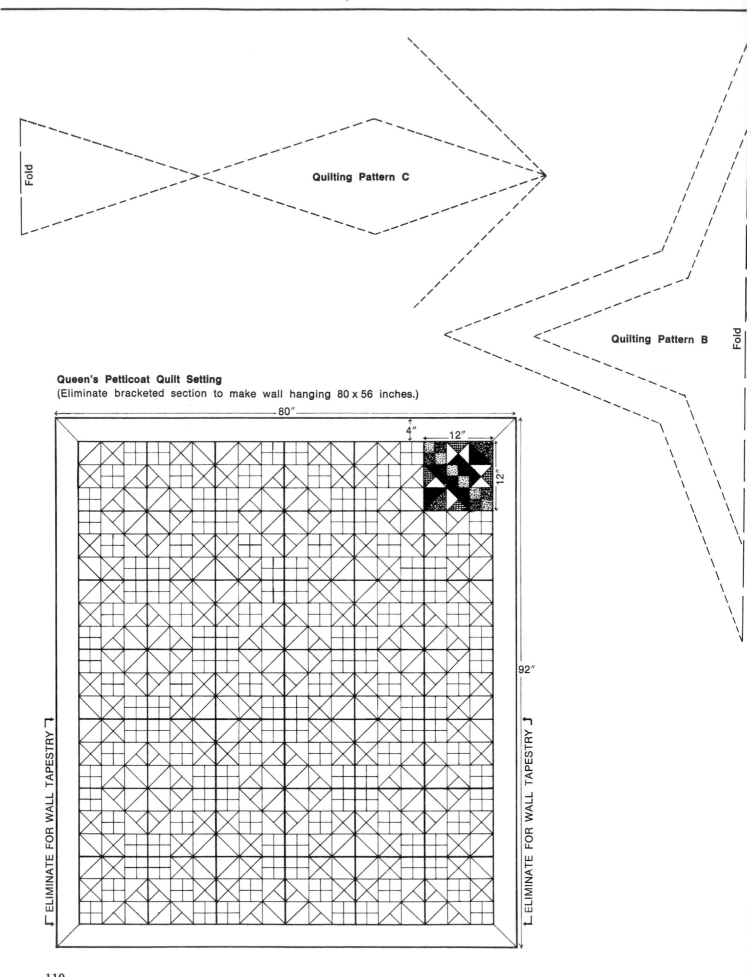

Fold

Quilting Pattern C

Quilting Pattern B

Fold

Queen's Petticoat Quilt Setting
(Eliminate bracketed section to make wall hanging 80 x 56 inches.)

80"

4"

12"

12"

92"

ELIMINATE FOR WALL TAPESTRY

ELIMINATE FOR WALL TAPESTRY

FLOWERING PLUM APPLIQUED
Shown on page 19

Materials: Tracing paper, black felt-tip pen, 13 sheets of white drawing paper 14 x 14 inches or white shelf paper 18 inches wide, matching sewing thread, bright yellow-orange embroidery floss, bonded polyester batting, ivory and gray-green quilting thread. See chart.

Finished quilt size is 78 x 86 inches.

Preparing patterns and templates: Copy the full-sized applique and corner patterns onto tracing paper and cut out. Rule a grid of 1 inch squares, 14 across and 14 down, onto white drawing or shelf paper. Draw a circle 14 inches in diameter on the grid of 1 inch squares. Following the drawing of the Flowering Plum design, arrange the actual-size paper patterns in position on the grid within the circle. The dotted lines on branch patterns No. 1, No. 2, No. 3, and No. 4 will match the grid lines when placed correctly. Pencil the outlines of each pattern piece onto the grid. Go over the pencil lines with black felt-tip pen and trace the reverse image of the design on the back of the paper as well.

To make working templates for each paper pattern, trace exact outlines onto cardboard or plastic and cut out carefully. Working with delicate branch patterns No. 1, No. 2, No. 3, and No. 4 will be easier if these are cut as stencil templates, and you'll be less likely to lose tiny pattern pieces No. 7, No. 8, No. 9, and No. 10 if these also are collected onto one stencil template.

Cutting binding, borders, blocks and corners: Cut the black fabric on the bias into strips 1½ inches wide; piece together to make 10 yards of quilt binding. Reserve the uncut

Cotton Fabric	36 inches wide	45 inches wide	
rosy pink	½ yd.		buds and flowers
black	1 yd.		calyxes and binding
dark gray	¾ yd.		branches
ivory	11 yds.	7½ yds.	applique blocks and lining
gray-green	6 yds.	4½ yds.	borders, blocks and corners

fabric for calyx appliques.

From the gray-green fabric, cut the borders first: two side borders, each 70¾ x 4¾ inches; a top and bottom border, each 78¾ x 8¾ inches. (If using 36 inch fabric, cut four strips 36 x 4¾ inches and piece to make the two side borders.) Next, cut 13 blocks, each 14¾ x 14¾ inches. Finally, cut 48 corners: for each corner, trace the outline of template No. 11 onto the wrong side of the fabric with sharply pointed pencil and cut an even ⅜ inch outside the pencilled line.

Cut 12 blocks, each 14¾ x 14¾ inches, from the ivory fabric.

Note: All piecing seam allowances are ⅜ inch. Each piece must be measured accurately and cut precisely if the parts are to fit together properly during final assembly.

Preparing blocks for applique: Cut white shelf or drawing paper into 12 squares 14 x 14 inches. On each square, draw a circle 14 inches in diameter. With black felt-tip pen, trace an image of the Flowering Plum design inside each circle, turning and reversing the design to duplicate the 12 variations specified by the diagrammed quilt setting.
Place a block of ivory fabric

face down on a flat surface. Center one of the Flowering Plum designs-on-paper face down over the fabric with the fabric's ⅜-inch seam allowance exposed all around. Pin and baste fabric and paper together around the outside edges. Turned right side up, the outlines on the paper will be visible through the fabric indicating where each applique should be stitched. Add extra basting around the branch design to hold the fabric against the paper.

In the same manner, baste a paper drawing to the remaining 11 fabric blocks. If your ivory block fabric is too opaque for the outlines to show through adequately, trace the Flowering Plum design directly onto the fabric with faint lines using a hard drawing pencil. Hold fabric and drawing over window glass; daylight from outside will reveal the lines for easy tracing. Baste blank paper to the fabric.

Cutting appliques:

For each appliqued block, you'll need:

Pattern	Cut	Fabric Color
Branch No. 1	1	gray
Branch No. 2	1	gray
Branch No. 3	1	gray
Branch No. 4	1	gray
Flower No. 5	2	pink

Pattern	Cut	Fabric Color
Flower No. 6	1	pink
Calyx No. 7	1	black
Petal No. 8	2	pink
Bud No. 9	4	pink
Calyx No. 10	4	black

(plus 4 of the corners you've already cut from the gray-green fabric.)

Trace the outlines of each applique template onto the right side of the appropriate fabric, tucking the sharp point of a pencil against the edge of the template. Arrange branch templates No. 1, No. 2, No. 3, and No. 4 along the bias of the fabric. Mark lightly on the pink fabric, heavily on the gray and black. Adding ⅛ inch seam allowance outside the pencilled fold-under line, cut out each applique with a small sharp scissors.

Sewing appliques: Matching the lines pencilled on the applique to the identical outlines that show through the fabric from the paper beneath, pin branch No. 1 in place on a block. With a single-threaded needle, begin at the base of the branch with a tiny back-stitch where it will be hidden by a subsequent applique. Fold the seam allowance under and pinch-crease on the pencilled line for an inch or so along the edge of the branch applique to be sewn down. Matching the folded edge to the line showing through the fabric, blindstitch the applique to the fabric. Stitch closely, 1/16 inch to ⅛ inch apart, pulling the thread taut after every five or six stitches to hold the applique firmly to the background fabric. Use the paper lining as a control to prevent excessive seam tension from drawing on the fabric. Continue pinch-creasing ahead, matching the folded edge to the outline and

blindstitching the applique to the background fabric, using the tip of the needle to urge reluctant seam allowances underneath and tease unwilling curves into smoothness. See illustration.

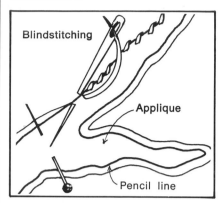

Roll and fold the paper-lined block so you can hold it comfortably in your hand, or bunch the paper in your hand as you would if the fabric weren't lined; the paper will wrinkle and crease, but it won't disintegrate. When sewing, allow the surface of the paper to deflect the needle back into the fabric, but if you should sew through the paper, it won't matter, the paper will pull away from any stitching during removal.

Portions of an applique that will be covered by another applique won't need stitching. Cut and remove branch fabric just inside the area that will be covered by a flower or bud so that the gray won't show through the pink. With the exception of pronounced curves and angles, the bias-cut, narrow seam allowances of the branches and other appliques will turn under without clipping. Begin stitching very closely when approaching a curve, angle, or point, clipping into seam allowances around deep inside curves and sharp inside angles, shoving seam allowances underneath with the tip of the needle, trimming seam allowances if necessary at points, keeping a firm tension on the sewing thread to prevent fabric threads or seam allow-

ances from creeping out. Cut tiny notches out of the seam allowances around small circles, such as buds and flowers, so that seam allowances will lie flat under the appliques. To secure a seam, take two tiny backstitches where they will be hidden by the applique, run the needle back under the applique between applique and background fabric, bring it out ½ inch away and cut the thread where it surfaces. Thread ends contained under an applique won't feather out to show through the background fabric later.

After branch No. 1, stitch branch No. 2 in place, then No. 3 and No. 4, proceeding to the flowers and buds in order as they are numbered. Finish the block by blind-stitching the four corners (No. 11) that frame the design. Clip and fold under the curved edge seam allowance (you may need to copy the pencilled line from the back of each corner applique onto the front), stitching it over the circular line that shows through the fabric from the drawing beneath.

Embroidering the flower centers: With a large needle, punch holes in flower templates No. 5 and No. 6 at the start and stop of each radiating line. Pencil dots through the template holes onto each appliqued flower. Using two strands of yellow-orange embroidery floss in a needle, connect the dots with a series of straight stitches. Finish with French knots at the tip of each stitch. Start by popping the knot at the end of the thread through the paper to lodge behind the background fabric and applique; end by pushing the needle and thread through the paper lining to the back, scratching a hole in the paper to allow securing the thread with a backstitch, re-inserting the needle between applique and background fabric to emerge ½ inch away where the thread is cut.

Assembling the quilt top:
Remove the basting threads to release the paper lining from each finished block, gently tearing the paper away from any other stitching. Cut away the unnecessary layer of background fabric behind the appliqued corners. Place each block face down over extra padding on an ironing board and steam press.

Seam the 12 appliqued blocks and the 13 plain gray-green blocks together in five rows of five as the setting diagram indicates. Sew ⅜ inch inside the cut edge using the lines previously pencilled on the back of each appliqued corner as sewing guidelines. Seams may be hand or machine stitched. Seam the five rows together, matching seams that cross. Stitch a 4-inch border to each side. Seam 8-inch borders across the top and bottom.

Press seam allowances toward the plain blocks away from the ivory fabric. Round the four corners of the quilt top to reflect the curve of the circular Flowering Plum frames.

Quilting: Seam together three 2½-yard lengths of 36-inch ivory fabric, or two 2½-yard lengths of 45-inch fabric, to make a sheet large enough to line the quilt top. Press seam allowances open. Stretch the lining out on a flat surface, lay batting over the lining, spread the top over all and baste the three layers together for quilting in a frame or a hoop.

Copy the actual size quilting templates onto tracing paper. Using any method you prefer, mark the top for quilting when it is stretched taut in a frame or hoop. Quilt a block at a time, working from the center of the quilt out to the border. Quilt each Flowering Plum design

around the appliques and inside the circular frame as illustrated. The overall quilting pattern that densely covers the background inside the frames is optional. Carry the diagonal maze pattern out into the borders as illustrated, using the border template to make the lines on the top. Use quilting thread colors that blend into the ivory and gray-green fabric colors.

Binding: Remove all basting threads. Trim lining and batting ½ inch from the seamline around the outside edge of the borders. Stitching through all three layers, sew one edge of the binding to the front of the quilt all around the outside. Turn the binding over the edge of the quilt to the back, fold the binding seam allowance under and blindstitch to the quilt lining. The binding seam allowance is ¼ inch; the width of the finished binding is ½ inch.

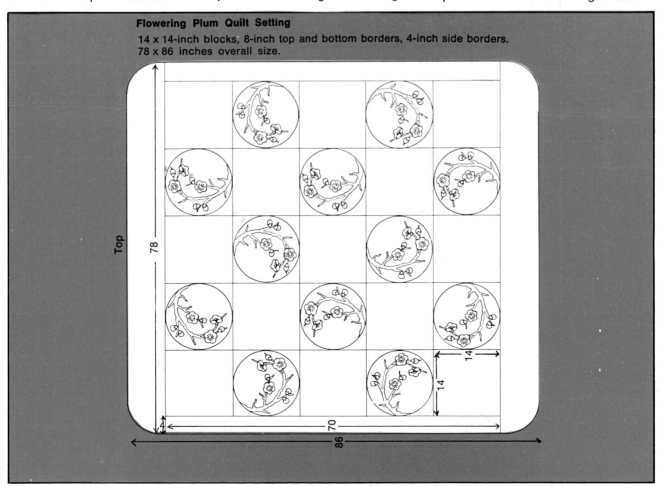

Flowering Plum Quilt Setting
14 x 14-inch blocks, 8-inch top and bottom borders, 4-inch side borders.
78 x 86 inches overall size.

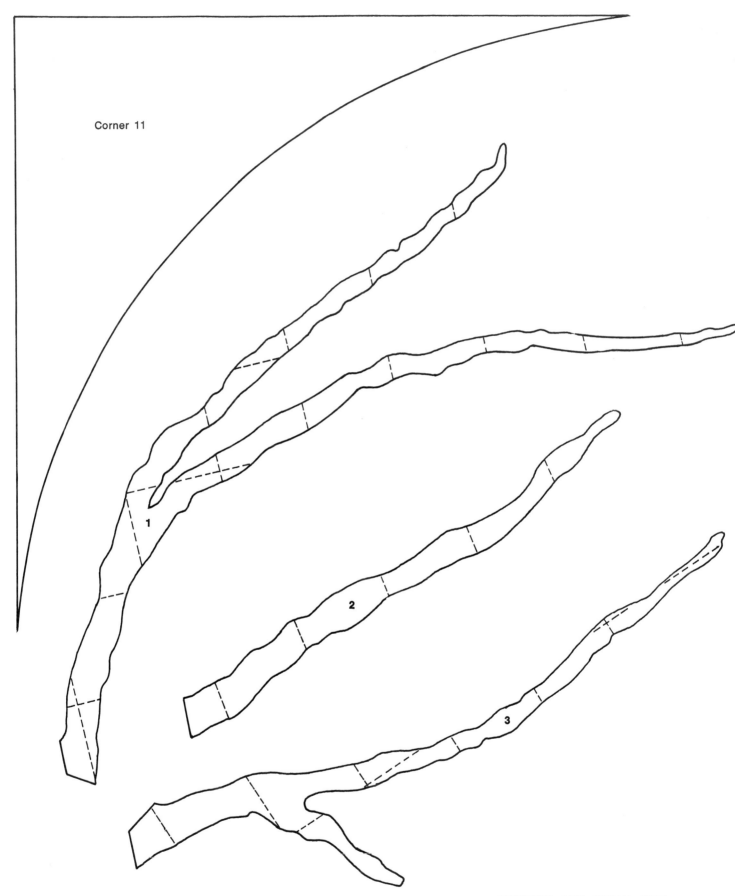

Corner 11

1

2

3

PATTERNS ARE ACTUAL SIZE

7

8

9

10

10

4

5

6

8

8

Quilting Pattern

Center of blocks

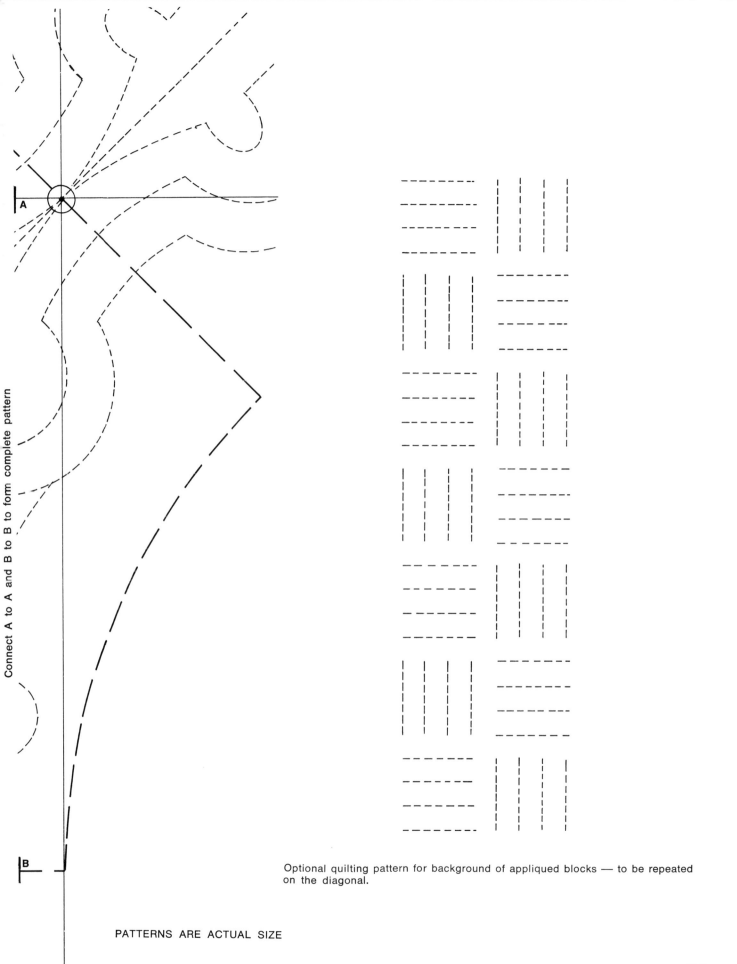

Connect A to A and B to B to form complete pattern

A

B

Optional quilting pattern for background of appliqued blocks — to be repeated on the diagonal.

PATTERNS ARE ACTUAL SIZE

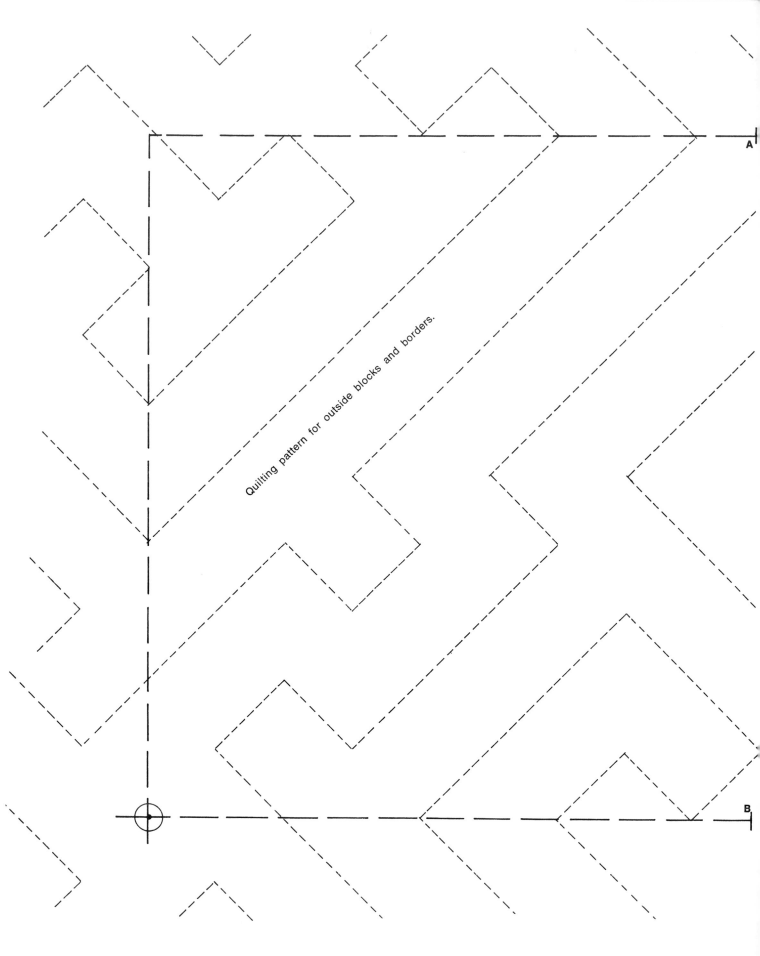

Quilting pattern for outside blocks and borders.

A

B

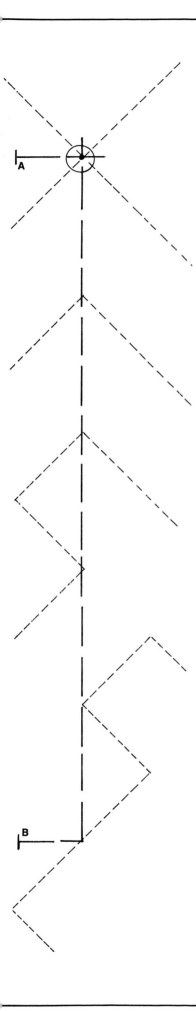

Diagram of quilt showing quilting; includes example of optional quilting in appliqued block.

EACH SQUARE EQUALS 1 INCH

HAWAIIAN FRUIT TREES
Shown on page 23

Materials: 10 yards 36-inch wide red cotton fabric; 1½ yards 45-inch wide red striped cotton fabric; ⅛ yard each of red, blue, yellow, green, orange and purple fabric; 2 yards boldly flowered 45-inch wide fabric; 2 yards 45-inch wide green cotton fabric; 4½ yards white fabric; quilting thread to match each color of fabric; quilt backing fabric; dacron or cotton quilt batt (very thin batt or omit entirely); wide white bias tape; tracing paper.

Finished size: 87 x 111 inches.

Note: Allow ¼ inch when cutting for seams.

Make templates and cut the following pieces:

144 round shapes ("fruit"): 24 from red, 24 from blue, 24 from yellow, 24 from green, 24 from orange and 24 from purple fabric.

All other parts of "tree" are cut from boldly flowered fabric: 24 of part A, 12 of part B, 12 of part C, 24 of part D, 24 of part E.

Cut 12 white blocks, 12 inches finished (allow ¼ inch all around when cutting).

Pattern placement: Draw entire pattern on thin tracing paper. Use this as a guide for placement of applique. Turn seams under on all pieces, baste. Using paper guide, place tree and fruit on each white block. Refer to color chart with pattern.

Pin or baste in place. For "fruit", using sewing machine or small hand stitches, make row of gathering threads around outer edge, pull gathers to form circle. Blindstitch all parts in place, except bottom of C. This edge will be covered by striped border. Use small stitches and matching thread.

Make very small stitches on points and inner corners. Insert small amount of dacron or cotton under fruit for padded effect. Complete twelve blocks in same manner.

Red and White striped border: Fold fabric diaperwise to get a true bias. Cut into 2-inch strips. Sew band to top and bottom of each white block, using ¼ inch seam. Join side stripes to block, matching top and bottom stripes exactly. Press all seams toward outer edges. Trim evenly.

Red border: Cut red fabric in strips and sew in place. Cut 24 strips, 6½ inches wide x 14½ inches long, 24 strips, 6½ inches wide x 27½ inches long. ¼-inch seam already allowed on these pieces. Sew 14½-inch red strip to sides of striped border on each block. Sew 27½-inch red strip to top and bottom of red striped border and red side band.

Green band: Cut fabric in sections 1½ yards each. Fold fabric diaper-wise to get a true bias. Cut into 2-inch widths. Sew green band to top of one red block, sew this green band to bottom of next red block. Join four blocks in this manner to form strip. There will be no green band at top and bottom of each strip. Join three strips

in this manner. Join three strips together with green bands lengthwise. There will be no green band on outer edge. When twelve blocks are joined together, sew green band to entire top and bottom edge and both sides, miter corners. This makes a green strip around each block.

Quilting: This is a large quilt, so batting may be omitted entirely or if used it should be very thin. Cut lining and batting, if used, same size as quilt top. With ruler and tailor's chalk, mark horizontal lines 1 inch apart on red bands, one being in seams. You may have to adjust slightly so space comes out evenly. This will not be noticed when quilt is completed. Pin and baste quilt top, batting if used and lining together. Use thread to match each section. Starting from center, quilt around center design, inner edge of white block, outer edge of red and white striped band, horizontal lines on red band, in the seam around green bands. Baste outer edge of quilt. Trim lining and batting even with top if necessary. With right sides together, using ¼-inch seam, sew bias tape around entire quilt. Turn to lining side, miter corners. Blindstitch in place. Green may be cut and used for this binding.

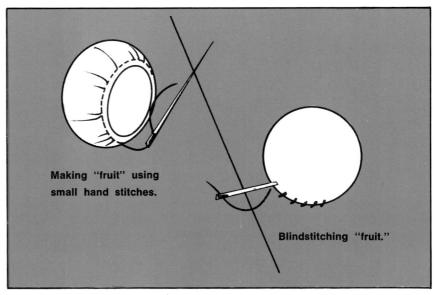

Making "fruit" using small hand stitches.

Blindstitching "fruit."

PATTERNS ARE ACTUAL SIZE

122

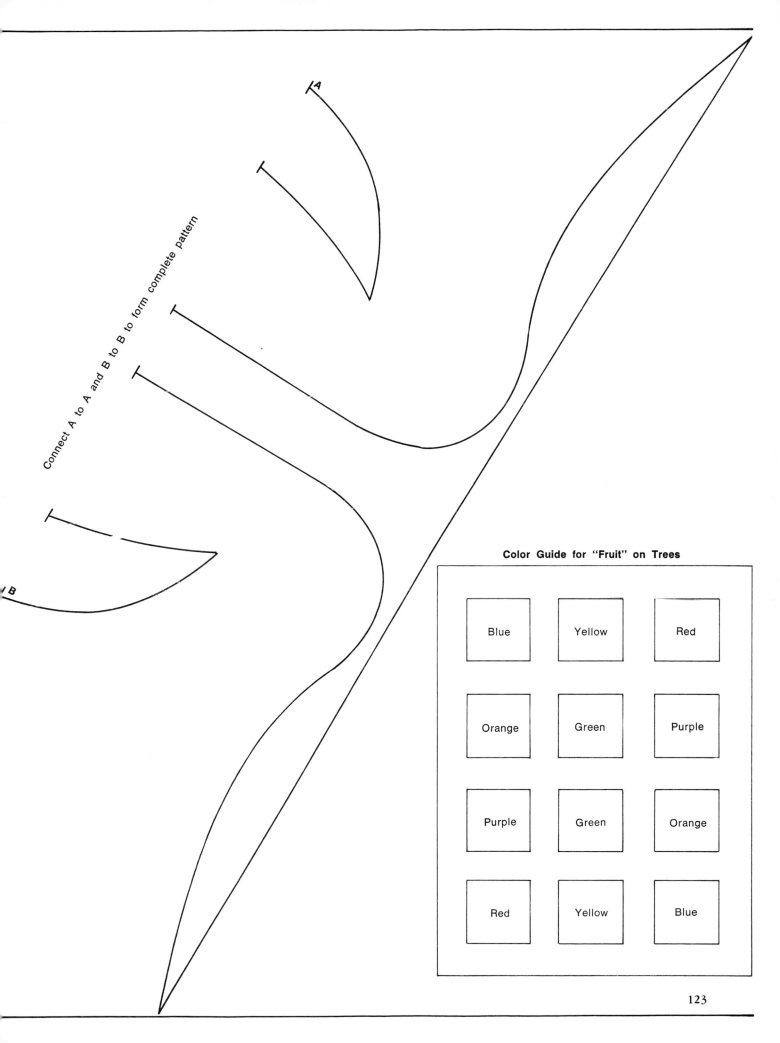

Connect A to A and B to B to form complete pattern

Color Guide for "Fruit" on Trees

Blue	Yellow	Red
Orange	Green	Purple
Purple	Green	Orange
Red	Yellow	Blue

STARS OVER HAWAII
Shown on page 25

Materials: One king-size yellow percale sheet for top of quilt, one king-size yellow muslin sheet for lining of quilt, one king-size polyester quilt batting (an additional piece may be needed), six yards of bright green fabric in one piece, 1½ yards of same green for making binding, four large spools of yellow quilting thread, two large spools of green quilting thread.

Finished quilt size: 99 x 99 inches.

Note: Rip out turned under hem of both edges of percale sheet and press with steam iron. Launder the muslin sheet after ripping out seams.

Mark the percale sheet in 1-inch squares with a pencil. These are the background quilt lines and must be done first as there is no way it can be done later. Enlarge the applique pattern and transfer to paper and cut out. Cut the six yards of green fabric in half and sew the two parts together. Press seams open, fold the fabric in half and then half again which makes it in four folds. Match centers of folds of pattern and fabric and place paper pattern on fabric after all four folds have been securely basted to prevent slipping.

Enlarge and pin paper pattern to fabric, then baste with long stitches and a long fine needle. This should be done about ½ inch from edge of pattern. With sharp scissors, cut through all four layers of fabric at one time. Use small scissors to cut out the different sizes of fish. Cut ⅛ inch from edge of pattern. Clear out a space on the floor so you can lay out the percale sheet flat and smooth. Open up the green fabric (from which you have just cut the design) and place it on the sheet according to

the pattern using the quilting lines as guides. Measure each leaf so each is the same distance from edges. Place the other stars as shown on pictured quilt. Baste ½ inch all around from the raw edges. It is not necessary to turn under edges and baste as this can be done in the final blind hand-finished stitching.

Using green thread, blindstitch around all appliques turning under ⅛ (or 1/16) inch as you go. Clip the curves of the fish as you proceed and buttonhole stitch all inner points and sharp curves. Embroider details on fish and flower cut outs.

Quilting: Cut yellow muslin sheet (lining) and batting same size as quilt top. Pin and baste quilt top, batting and lining together. Using yellow thread, quilt the pencil lines you drew on the yellow percale sheet. Do not quilt through the appliques, quilt only on the lines still visible. Quilt in the ditch around appliques. Baste outer edge of quilt, trim lining and batting even with top. Fold 1½ yard piece of green fabric diaper-wise and cut for binding in 1½-inch widths. Sew strips together as needed to bind quilt.

Sew binding to each side of quilt top. Miter corners. Fold binding over edge of quilt to back, hand finish.

ACTUAL SIZE

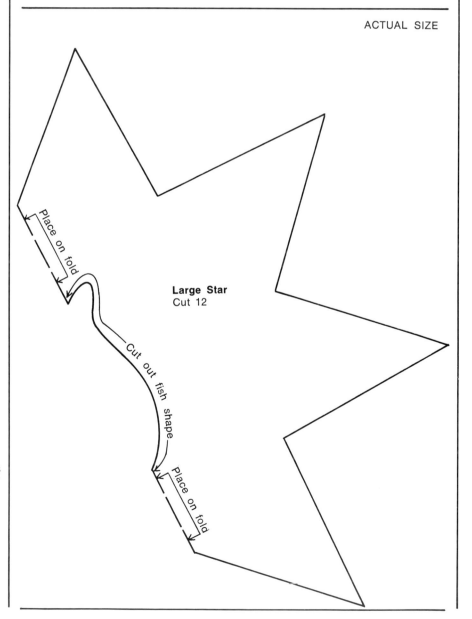

Place on fold

Cut out fish shape

Place on fold

Large Star
Cut 12

124

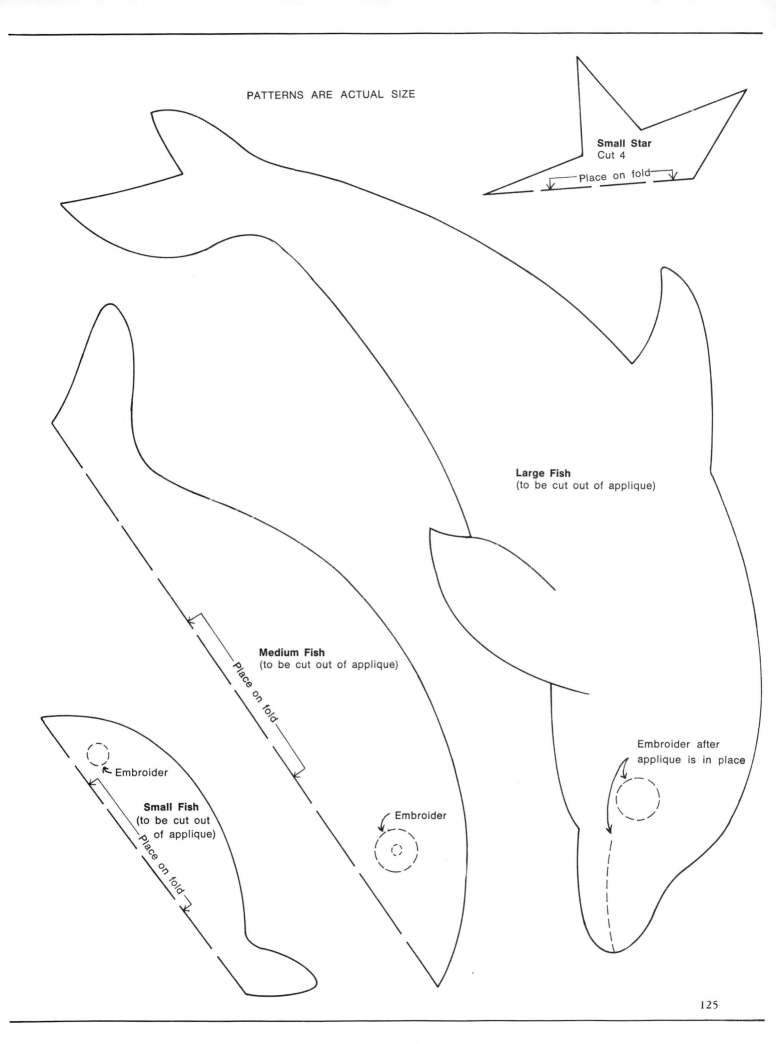

PATTERNS ARE ACTUAL SIZE

Small Star
Cut 4

Place on fold

Large Fish
(to be cut out of applique)

Medium Fish
(to be cut out of applique)

Place on fold

Embroider after
applique is in place

Embroider

Small Fish
(to be cut out
of applique)

Place on fold

Embroider

Place on fold

EACH SQUARE EQUALS 1 INCH

A

B

Embroider

Cut out

Stitch, don't cut

Cut out

Cut out

Cut out

Cut out

Stitch, don't cut

Center of fold

126

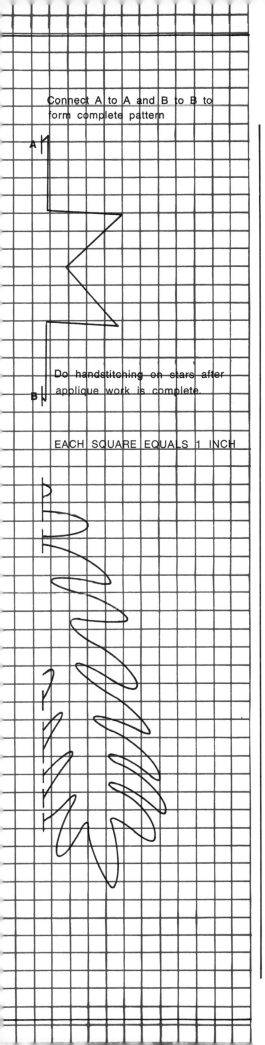

Connect A to A and B to B to form complete pattern

A

Do handstitching on stars after applique work is complete.

B

EACH SQUARE EQUALS 1 INCH

CHRISTMAS STAR
Shown on page 27

Materials: King-size white percale sheet (with all hems opened and pressed flat) or eight yards of 45-inch white polyester/cotton fabric for quilt top; five yards of 45-inch red cotton fabric for cutting appliques, borders and hems; red quilting thread to match, silver metallic thread for embroidery, white quilting thread; 22 skeins of DMC No. 321 red floss for backstitch quilting; king-size muslin sheet (with all hems opened and pressed flat) for lining; king-size polyester batting (check size, you may need to piece a strip to obtain proper size); graph paper (pieced together to form 30-inch square); thin white art paper or tracing paper; cardboard; white pencil; black lead pencil.

Size: Approximately 92 x 100 inches.

Note: No allowance made for seams. Allow ⅛-inch turn under allowance on large center star and star parts and ¼-inch allowance on all red stars and seams, unless otherwise specified in instructions.

Make a 30-inch square of graph paper. This is a must for a perfect block. With heavy black pen draw two diagonal lines from corner to corner and from center draw both horizontal and vertical lines. Between these lines mark off 1⅞-inch spaces and draw lines to center of square. There will be seven lines. The first lines (diagonal, horizontal and vertical) are guidelines for white quilting. From these, every other one will be for red backstitching which alternates with quilting stitches.

Place tracing paper over drawn graph paper block and trace entire pattern for use on quilt. All quilting lines must be drawn on fabric first before appliquing. It cannot be done successfully later.

If you are using a king-size sheet for quilt top, begin by placing the 30-inch marked block underneath, several inches from top and side and trace with pencil all quilting lines. Trace three blocks across, three blocks down for a total of nine blocks. The only other drawing will be the outside lines around all nine blocks. No other seamlines should be drawn and all quilting lines must meet each other exactly within all nine blocks. Allow ¼-inch for seams when cutting out extra fabric of sheet around the nine blocks.

If you are using fabric yardage for quilt top, use 30-inch marked block for a guide for a perfect square and when cutting blocks be sure to allow ¼-inch for seams. It is best to sew the blocks together by hand, matching all marked quilting lines, anchoring with pins first.

Applique: Cut off two yards (45 x 72 inches) from red fabric for parts (remainder will be for borders and binding). To cut the center star motif, fold 24 x 24-inch piece of red fabric twice to form a 12 x 12-inch square. This must be done exactly, so press each fold at a time and baste around edges after second fold. We have given the entire center star motif so you can see exactly how it should look when cut out, but you will only use ¼ of the pattern for cutting purposes as it is cut Hawaiian-style. Place the center of the ¼ pattern on the corner of the folded fabric. Open raw edges of red folded fabric will be at top and right side of folded square. Baste pattern to fabric through center star and within ½ inch of pattern edge. Do not remove these bastings until all cutting is complete. When cutting fabric, allow ⅛ inch all around for turn under when appliqueing. See illustration.

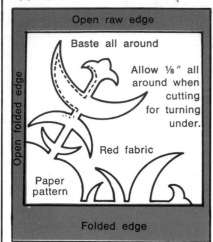

Place center star motif cut-out on center block of quilt top, lining it up horizontally and vertically with marked lines on block. Baste in place. Turn under ⅛-inch hem as you blindstitch the motif to the block.

Cut out six (you will cut 26 in all) small stars from red fabric, allowing ¼-inch all around and applique in place as indicated on center star motif pattern. Buttonhole stitch all inner and outer points of applique work except for small stars which need only the inner points buttonholed.

From red fabric, cut out eight star part motifs and arrange on quilt matching top of star part with intersection of quilting lines in center of block, lining up bottom points of parts with straight ilnes of vertical corners or center horizontal and vertical lines of block. See quilt diagram. Two small stars are appliqued in position indicated on quilt diagram, one on each side of each star part motif (16 stars). Four small stars are appliqued on the four inter-sections where all nine blocks meet.

To make border of quilt: From the remaining red fabric cut four strips 7 x 92 inches (two are for top and bottom border and two will be used for quilt binding later). Cut two strips 2½ x 104 inches for side

borders and two strips 3 x 104 inches for side binding (bind-ing pieces to be used later).

Top and bottom 7-inch borders are sewn on quilt first (½-inch seams, right sides together) and can be done on sewing machine. Trim on sides. Press seams toward red. Then attach 2½-inch side borders (¼-inch seams, right sides together) which go to top and bottom of quilt including top and bottom borders. Trim. See illustration.

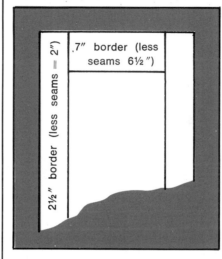

Marking the border for quilting: Make cardboard patterns of cross, crown and calvary steps. The first cross is drawn even with the side border, ½ inch down from top of quilt, then draw crosses 1 inch apart across top border ending with the last one even with the opposite side border seam. There are three crowns drawn in between the crosses 3 inches down from top of quilt: the first is between the first and second crosses, the second is between the 11th and 12th crosses and the third is between the last two crosses at the other end of the border. The steps of Calvary are drawn 4 inches down from top of quilt, beginning in between the third and fourth crosses and all other crosses for a total of nine up to the center crown, then nine times on the other side. The symbols of Christmas are the two X's, 5 inches in length drawn 1 inch down from top

of quilt. They are on side border even with first cross and last cross, close to seam line. See illustration.

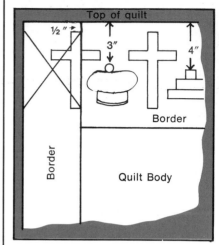

Assembling quilt: Use king-size polyester batting (a narrow addition may be necessary to length of batting; use white thread and double overcasting stitch to attach). Open hems of king-size sheet (for lining) and launder. Lay the lining on the floor, then batting, then appliqued quilt top, right side up. Baste all three layers together with double thread all around. Do not cut off extra fabric of lining as this is useful when anchoring in hoop.

Quilting: Begin quilting with Christmas Star in center of quilt. First, pull quilt up taut in hoop and backstitch (with two strands of red floss) all lines in center circle of motif. Using cardboard template of star, punch hole in center and line up with center point of lines and outline, first with pencil, then remove cardboard template and backstitch with silver thread. Embroider silver star with solid satin stitches, completely covering outline stitches. Embroider a silver tip on four stars at intersections of center block using a satin stitch. Loosen up quilt in hoop and quilt in white thread all other quilting which includes around applique, parts, stars and quilting lines, remembering that the beginning line of white quilting is the vertical, horizontal or diagonal line, reserving the alternating ones for red backstitching, to be done after white quilting. When backstitching with red, have quilt very taut in hoop. Proceed downward and outward until all white quilting is complete. Then complete all backstitching in red.

Note: By keeping quilt very taut in hoop when doing backstitching and very loose when doing other quilting which is simply running stitches, gives a combination of light and shadow and makes for a more interesting quilt.

Border quilting: Cross and Calvary steps are quilted in red thread. Crowns and X's are done in backstitch using silver thread.

Binding: Attach the 7-inch red binding strips to top and bottom of quilt using ½-inch seams, right sides together (may be sewn on machine). Turn down ½-inch hem on top of side border at the same time. Turn and press seams toward red border. Turn under ½-inch

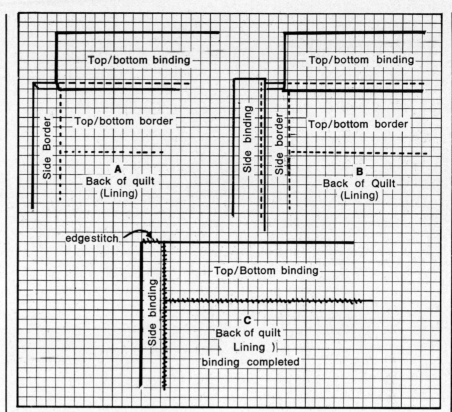

hem, press; turn to back of quilt and blindstitch to quilt lining. Do the same with the **side 3-inch binding using ¼-inch seam allowance.** Turn back ½-inch hem, press (edge-

stitch around if desired), turn to back of quilt and blindstitch to quilt lining. The narrow binding will cover raw side edges of top binding when it is turned to back of quilt.

PATTERNS ARE ACTUAL SIZE

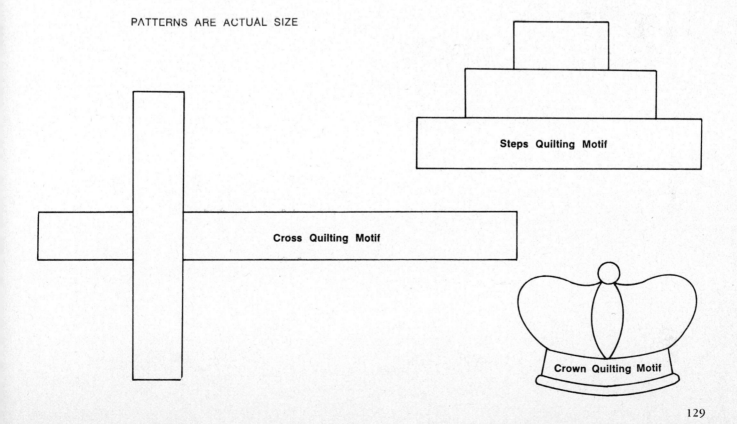

Steps Quilting Motif

Cross Quilting Motif

Crown Quilting Motif

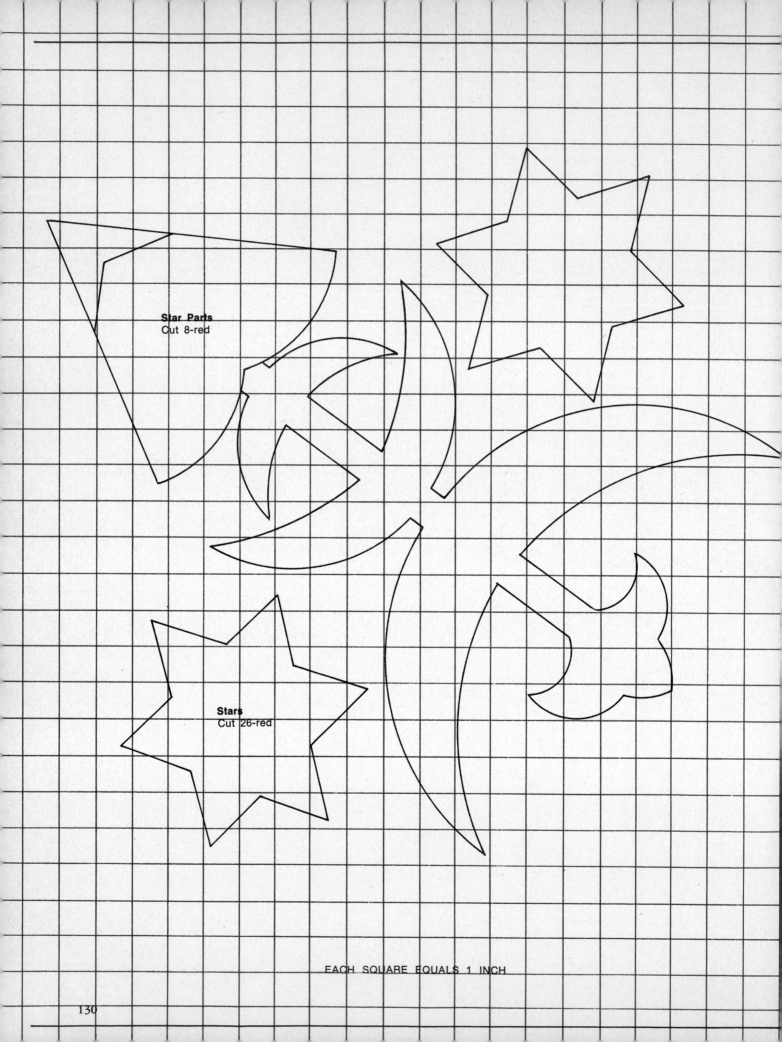

Star Parts
Cut 8-red

Stars
Cut 26-red

EACH SQUARE EQUALS 1 INCH

Large Center Star Motif
(Fold to ¼, place on doubled fabric and cut Hawaiian or doily style)

Stars are for placement only and should be cut separately.

EACH SQUARE EQUALS 1 INCH

----- Quilting lines. Do not cut!

131

· · · · · · · · · · white quilting lines

─ ─ ─ ─ ─ red backstitching lines

SUNSTAR
Shown on page 29

Materials: Cotton/poly fabric in the following colors and amounts: 4 yards red, 5 yards yellow, 3 yards blue; 6 yards red backing fabric; quilting thread to match each color, polyester quilt batt.

Finished size: 82⅜ x 99½ inches.

The quilt is made up of twelve squares, each composed of four Parts A (yellow), four Parts B (blue), four Parts C (yellow), four Parts D (blue) and one red star. Add ¼-inch seam allowance to all pattern parts when cutting out.

Note: Part A is partially covered by points of star on pattern. It is an 8 x 6-inch rectangle. The pattern shows the results of placing the star in position which partially covers each part A.

To assemble squares: Attach one Part B to each side of Part A. Do this twice.

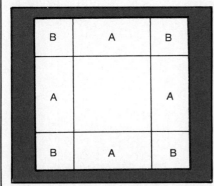

Attach A lengthwise to ends of these strips.

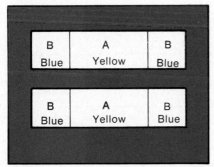

Attach Part C to both sides of square.

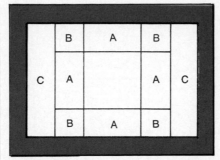

Attach Part D to ends of two more Part C's.

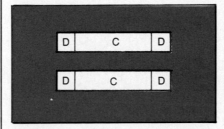

Attach C/D strips to top and bottom of assembled square.

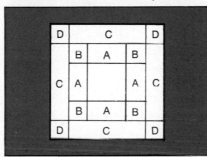

Attach red star, which has been prepared by turning under seams and pressing, to center of assembled square matching all seams. The points of the star should be at the top edge of Parts A.

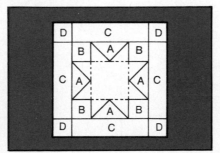

Make twelve blocks in this manner.

After twelve blocks are completed, sew three blocks together with 1-inch strips (¼-inch seam allowance on each side) between each block. Measure your completed block

for accurate measurement for length of red strip.

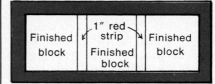

Sew 1½-inch red strip (with ¼-inch seam allowance on each side for a 1-inch finished strip) across bottom of these three blocks.

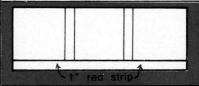

Sew three more finished blocks together with 1-inch red strips (¼-inch seam allowance) as for first three blocks. Sew the two rows of three blocks together.

Sew 1-inch red strips (¼-inch seam allowance) across bottom of second row of blocks. Continue in this manner until 12 blocks are joined together with 1-inch red strips.

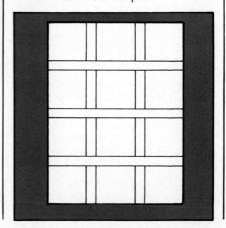

133

Quilt top is now complete. Place in quilt frame with polyester quilt batt and red backing fabric 1¼ inch larger all around than finished quilt top to allow for turning to front for binding. Or have quilt backing fabric same size if binding separately.

Quilting: Yellow Parts C are quilted in a zigzag.

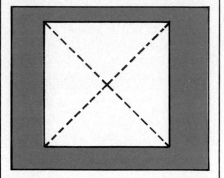

Blue Parts B and D are quilted in an X.

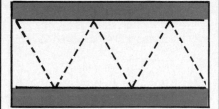

Quilt stars according to dotted radial lines on star pattern. The yellow triangular shapes between points of stars are quilted with straight lines ¼ inch apart.

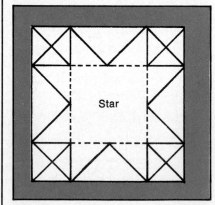

Finishing: If quilt is to be self-bound, turn backing fabric to front for a 1-inch binding, turn under ¼ inch and blind-stitch. Or, cut red strips on the bias to give a 1-inch binding and sew all around quilt.

Piecing and Quilting Diagram for Sunstar

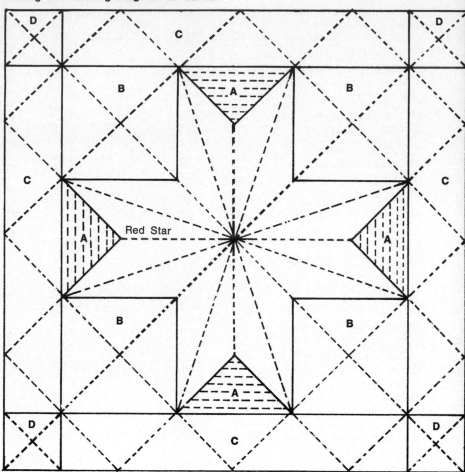

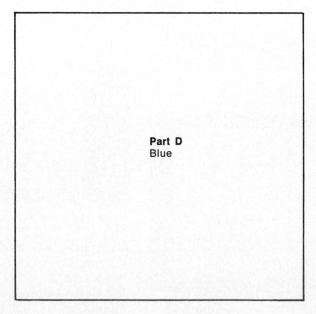

Part D
Blue

PATTERNS ARE ACTUAL SIZE

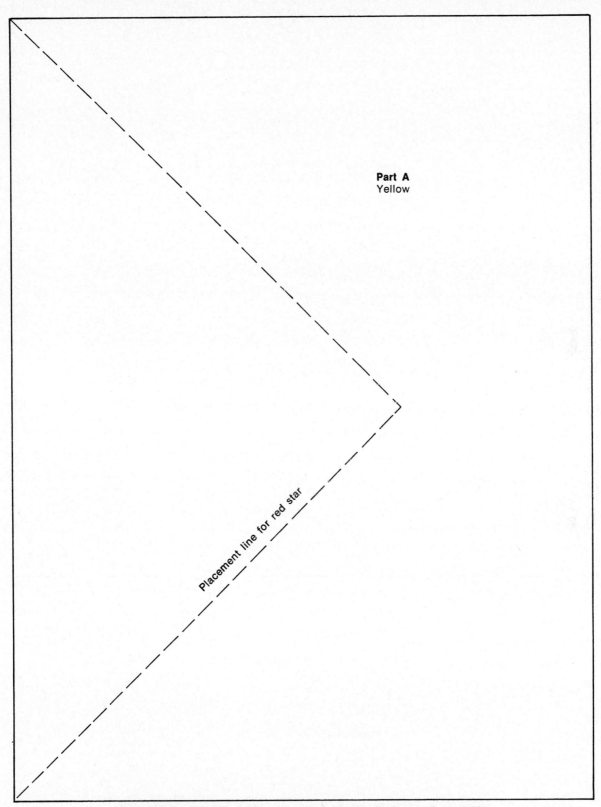

Part A
Yellow

Placement line for red star

For machine piecing: Add seam allowances to all pieces when making templates. The pencil line will be your cutting line.
For hand piecing: Do not add seam allowances to pieces when making templates. Add seam allowance when cutting fabric. The pencil line will be your sewing line.

Part B
Blue

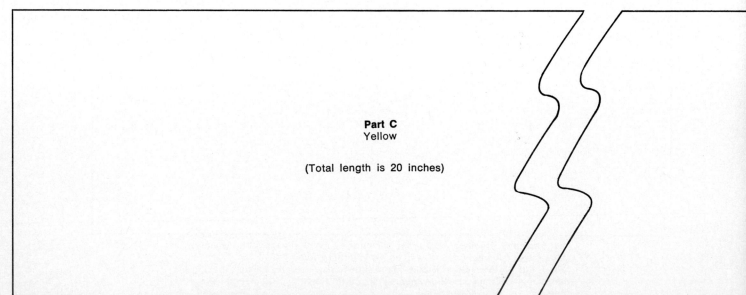

Part C
Yellow

(Total length is 20 inches)

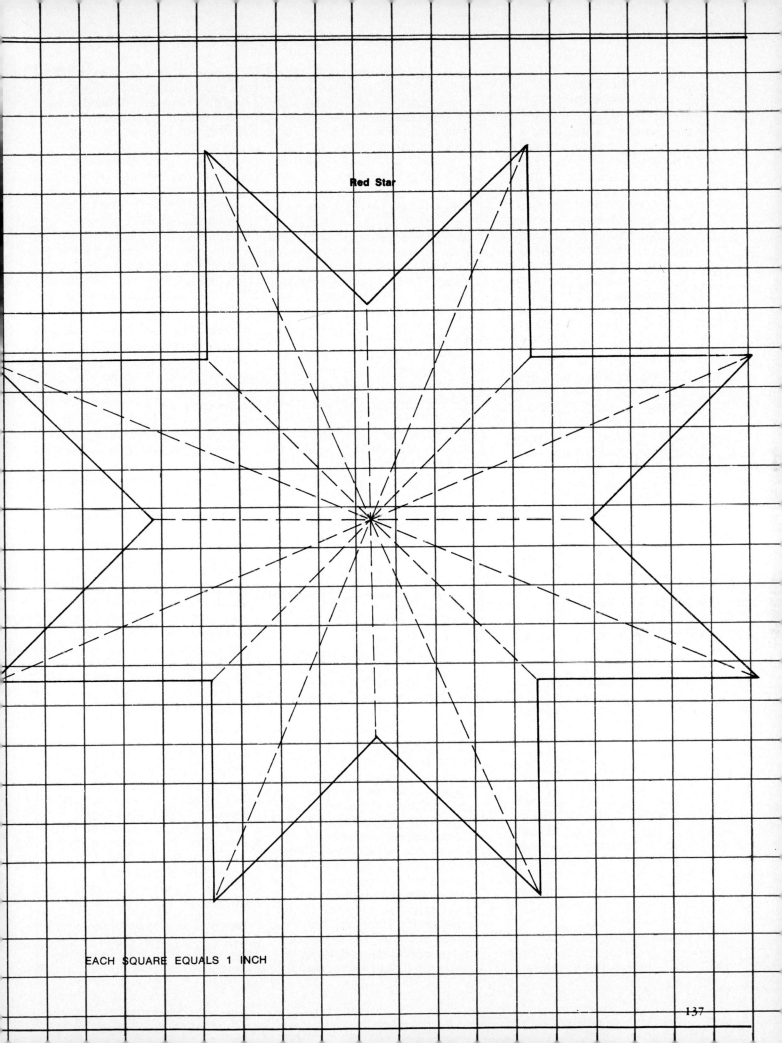

Red Star

EACH SQUARE EQUALS 1 INCH

ALONG THE RIVER
Shown on page 31

Materials: 5½ yards dark bright green fabric; 5½ yards lime green fabric; 4½ yards dark brown fabric; 3 yards brown flowered print fabric; 3 yards bright light blue fabric; two packages blue 1-inch seam binding; two packages light green 1-inch seam binding; thread to match all fabrics; border fabrics: 2/3 yard lime green fabric; 2/3 yard light blue fabric. No batting used.

Finished quilt is 92 x 88 inches. 48 blocks, six wide and eight long.

Cut 48 blocks from dark green material each 11½ x 14½ inches. (¼ inch for seams all around as block must by 11 x 14 inches finished.) Make a cardboard template of each part. Cut 48 Part A — lime green. Cut 48 Part B — dark brown. Cut 48 Part C — brown flowered print. Cut 48 Part D — light blue.

Turn under ¼-inch seams and baste all pieces except narrow edges of lime green which are left raw edges and short ends of blue which are left open and raw edges. Clip the curves on Part D (the blue river) when turning under the ¼-inch hem for basting.

Assembling quilt blocks: Place Part A (lime green) on green block first, centering exit of river (ends left open) with center of green block on both sides, baste. Place Part B (dark brown) on top of Part A so that spaces are even all around, baste. On these two place Part C (brown flowered print). Space evenly, baste. Lastly, and on top of all, place Part D (light blue) crosswise block. Center blue with center of green block at seams, but leave ends open, basting only sides of blue.

Finishing: Beginning with the outer layer (lime green) hand finish (blindstitch) to layer underneath, blindstitch B, C and D to layers underneath using same color thread, leaving ends of blue (Part D) and ends of lime green (Part A) open. These must have raw edges to match the green block and sewed up with the green edges.

When the entire block is all hand finished, turn it to the wrong side. Holding the outside layer (Blue Part D) out, carefully cut away the dark green block material to ¼ inch of stitching. Then cut away the lime green materials (Part A) to ¼ inch of stitching, then the brown flowered materials (Part B). The remainder can be left intact as these thicknesses would not be too great to quilt through. By eliminating all excess materials, you will find the quilting a much easier job. See illustration.

Making each block in layers and cutting out the excess from the back makes it easier to assemble, makes it more perfect, and many times faster to hand finish. See illustration.

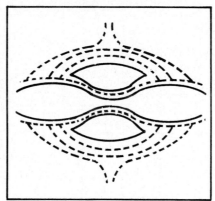

To assemble, sew six blocks together, horizontally for eight rows. First center the raw edges of the blue river and pin, then baste together so they meet exactly. Using blue thread backstitch by hand. Then baste remainder of green block, and hand finish the same way. Repeat until six blocks are joined. After eight rows are made, then sew them together the same way, only this time, first center the raw edges of the lime green and using matching thread hand sew securely. Then match seams of all green blocks and secure together. Proceed to hand finish remainder of green blocks with back stitches. If it is necessary to stretch one side or the other to make them come out evenly, do this by tiny clipping on the shorter side and stretch. It won't hurt it a bit as long as your hand stitching is tiny and firm. This is one quilt that is best done entirely by hand because of the careful matching of parts that must be done to look the very best.

Border: The sides of the quilt border are blue as the blue of the river flows this way. The ends of the quilt border are lime green because the subsidiary of the river flows this way. Fold the 2/3 yard of each color diaperwise and cut in strips 4 inches wide and sew together to length needed to border quilt. Sew to quilt top, mitering corners.

Quilting: Using 1¼ inches as guide, draw lines on either side of the blue river (Part D) across entire quilt, following the curves, and into the border, and using the same method and width of space draw the curved lines uniformly. Gently curve the lines from the exit of the green of the quilt block into the curve of the border. Beginning with the outer edges of the green squares, mark off quilting lines about 1 inch apart evenly around curves until they meet in diamond-like shapes. These might vary a little so it might be necessary to add a little or detract from this 1-inch space. Just match them as closely as posible. Use this same method on the curves of the border. Quilt in the ditch around A, B, C, D. Ripple-effect quilting is worked in the borders using quilting templates as guides.

Use blue seam binding to bind sides of quilt and green seam binding to bind top and bottom of quilt.

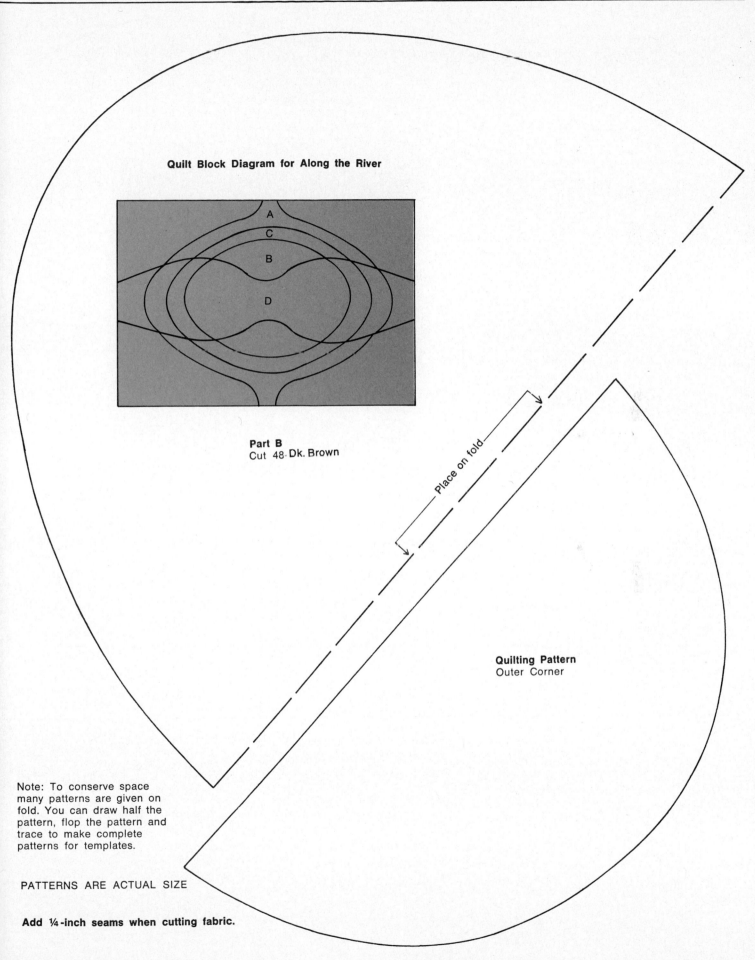

Quilt Block Diagram for Along the River

Part B
Cut 48-Dk. Brown

Place on fold

Quilting Pattern
Outer Corner

Note: To conserve space
many patterns are given on
fold. You can draw half the
pattern, flop the pattern and
trace to make complete
patterns for templates.

PATTERNS ARE ACTUAL SIZE

Add ¼-inch seams when cutting fabric.

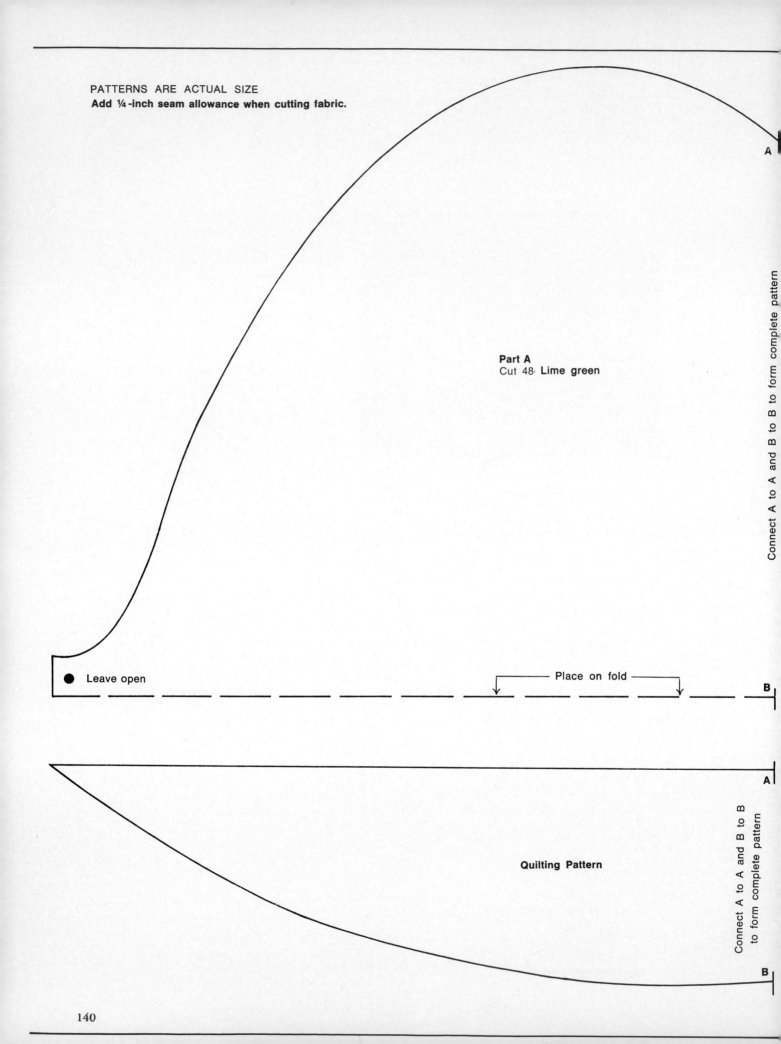

PATTERNS ARE ACTUAL SIZE
Add ¼-inch seam allowance when cutting fabric.

A

Connect A to A and B to B to form complete pattern

Part A
Cut 48· **Lime green**

● Leave open

Place on fold

B

A

Connect A to A and B to B to form complete pattern

Quilting Pattern

B

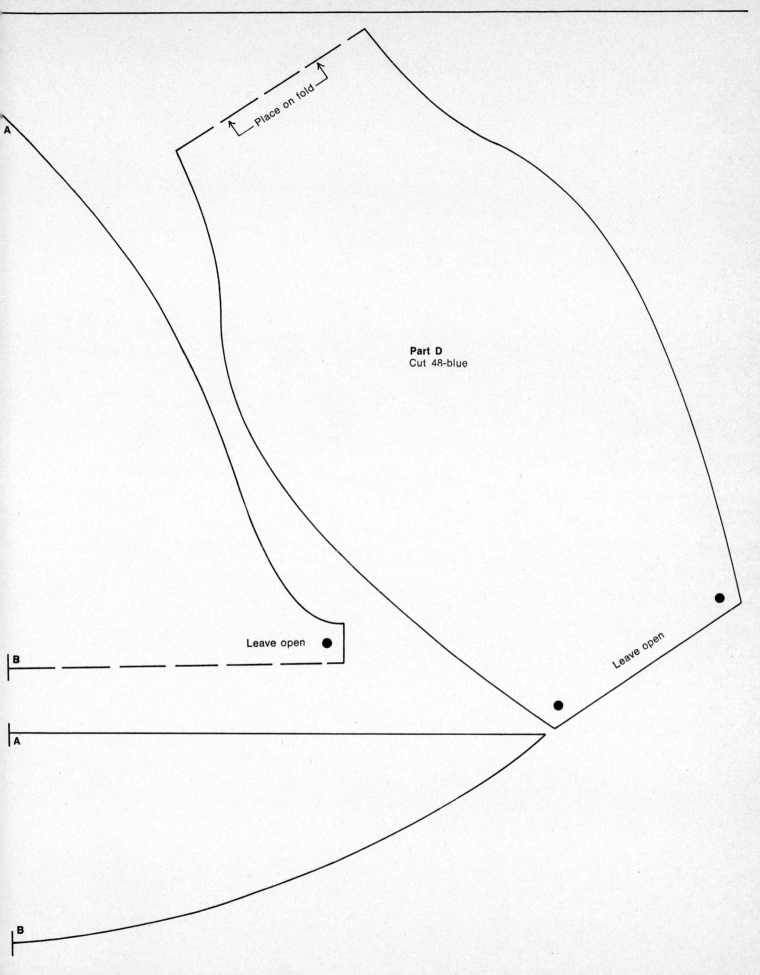

A

Place on fold

Part D
Cut 48-blue

B

Leave open ●

A

Leave open

●

●

B

141

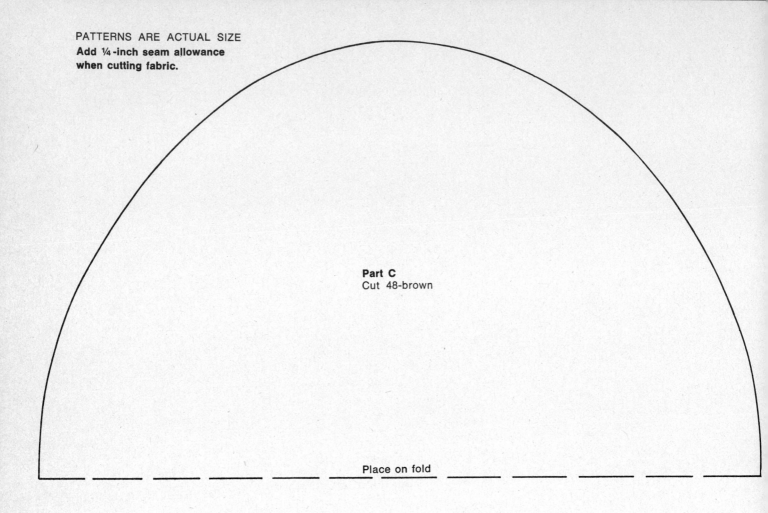

PATTERNS ARE ACTUAL SIZE
Add ¼-inch seam allowance when cutting fabric.

Part C
Cut 48-brown

Place on fold

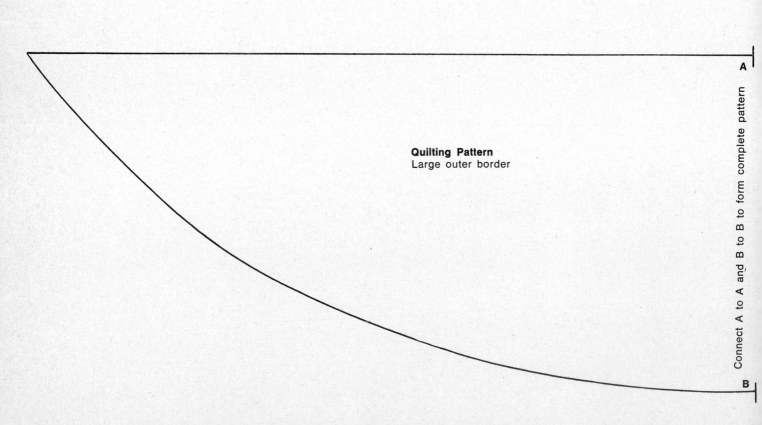

Quilting Pattern
Large outer border

A

B

Connect A to A and B to B to form complete pattern

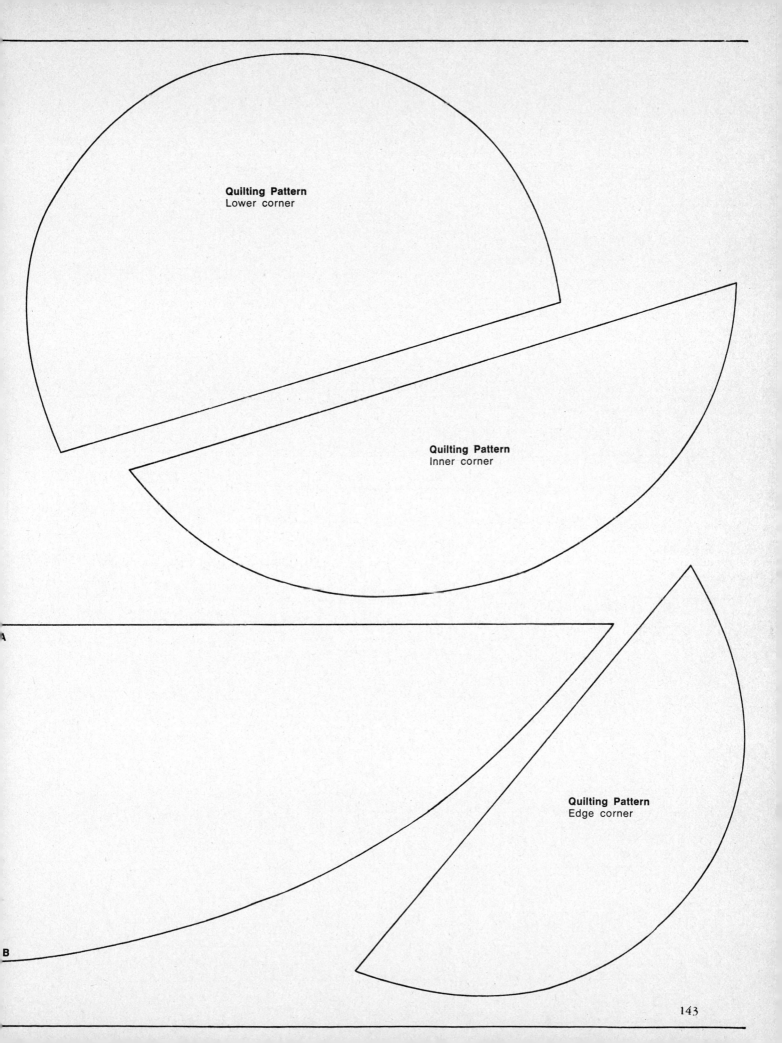

Quilting Pattern
Lower corner

Quilting Pattern
Inner corner

Quilting Pattern
Edge corner

A

B

143

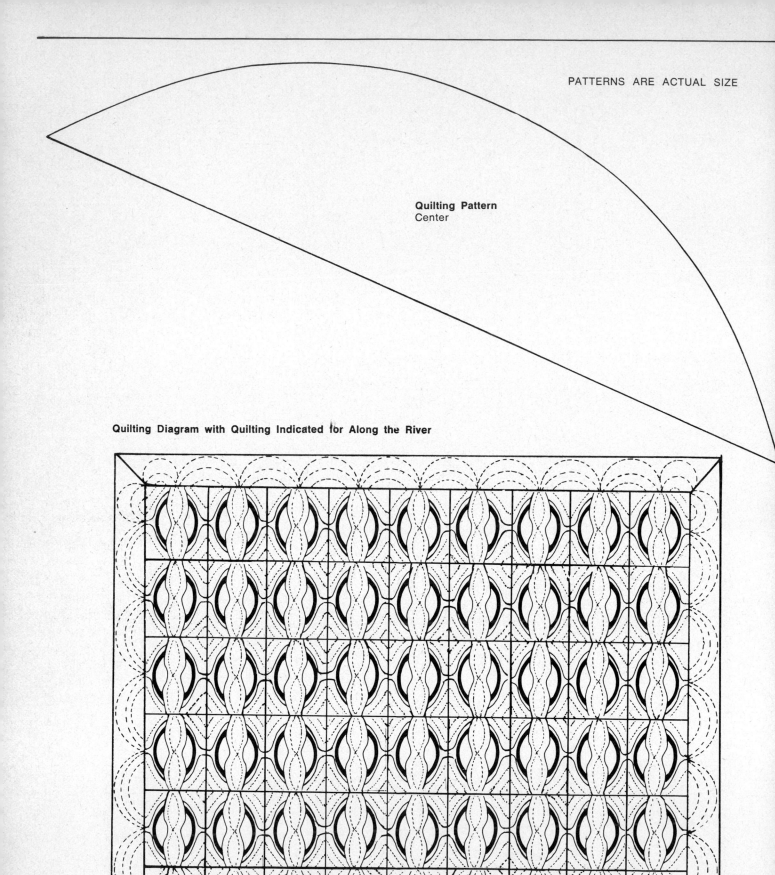

Quilting Pattern
Center

Quilting Diagram with Quilting Indicated for Along the River

COUNTRY ROSE
Shown on page 33

Materials: 45-inch cotton or cotton blend fabric in the following colors and amounts: 6 yards bright pink, 9 yards white, 1 yard yellow, 1¼ yards green; polyester batting; polyester stuffing; yellow perle cotton, pink perle cotton; king-size sheet or fabric yardage for quilt lining.

Finished size: 104 x 120 inches.

The quilt is made up of 63 blocks, (seven blocks wide and nine blocks long), each 13 inches square (12 inches finished), plus a 10-inch border on sides and bottom with 2-inch pink binding at top of quilt.

The quilt is made in vertical strips. The designs are arranged so they correspond to each other on every other strip.

Four blocks form the pattern of the quilt as shown below.

The four-block pattern is repeated 3½ times across the top, beginning and ending with a pink flower. It is repeated 4½ times top to bottom also beginning and ending with a pink flower. See quilt diagram with pattern.

The large pink flowers represent the full blooms, the small green flowers represent the bud and the small pink flowers represent the opening bud. The opening bud has three rows of quilting ½ inch apart to indicate the movement of the opening bud. Pink opening buds fall directly under pink full blooms while green buds fall at "corners" of full blooms.

Make cardboard templates of each pattern piece. Cut five large pink petals for each of the 32 full blooms (160 petals), adding ¼ inch seam allowance. Cut five more for each bloom with no seam allowance (160). Cut 32 yellow centers adding seam allowances — one for each of the full blooms; cut

five small petals for each of the 21 opening buds (155) and cut five small petals for each of the 48 green buds (240).

Note: You need ten petals for each full bloom because the pink petals need to be double or two layers so that the yellow center fabric will not show through.

To make the 32 full bloom blocks, position the yellow center in the center of 13-inch block. Position five pink petals (from the ones cut ¼ inch smaller) as shown on diagram with patterns. Anchor these in place with pink thread. Applique the top five petals in place using blindstitch. Each petal is anchored to the other.

To make the 31 opening bud blocks, use center guide circle and position five petals around it as shown on four-block diagram. Applique the petals in place using blindstitch, leaving an opening and stuffing each petal with a small amount of stuffing and then closing with blindstitches. Anchor stuffing on back with basting stitches. Embroider the center with yellow French knots.

Join the blocks, seven across and nine top to bottom, alternating vertical strips to form pattern as shown in quilt diagram. At the seam junctions you will applique the green buds in place, centering them on the seam line crossing. You can applique these buds as you join four blocks together. The centers of the green buds are satin stitched in pink perle cotton.

Join a 10-inch white border to bottom and sides of quilt and a 2-inch pink border to the top of the quilt. (If you choose, the 10-inch white border can also go across the top.)

Place quilt lining, batting and quilt top together and baste.

Quilt in the ditch around each large petal, yellow center, small green petal and small pink petal. Quilt around each pink opening bud three times, ½ inch apart as shown on

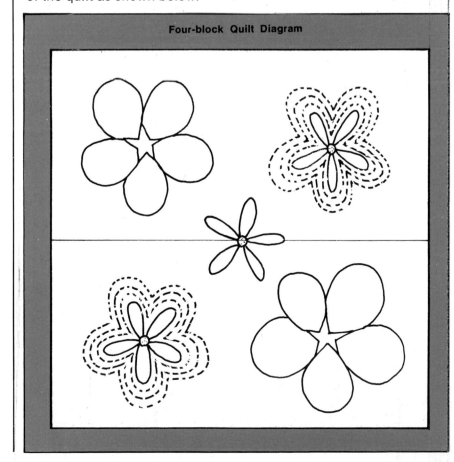

Four-block Quilt Diagram

diagram with patterns. Make a
template of small petal ¼ inch
smaller all around and use it to
quilt a petal shape in between
each petal of the green buds.
Quilt the border in rows 1 inch
apart horizontally and then
quilt double vertical lines (½
inch apart) every 12 inches.
The border quilting indicates
a country fence.
Bind quilt with white yardage
or seam binding or blindstitch
all around to lining.

PATTERNS ARE ACTUAL SIZE

Add ¼-inch seam allowance when cutting fabric

Yellow Centers
Cut 32

✕
Center

Large Pink Petal

Cut 5 for each bloom for 32 blooms,
adding seam allowance (160). Cut 5
more for each bloom (160) with no
seam allowance to line petals.

**Small Pink &
Green Petals**

Cut 5 for each bud:
31 pink buds (155)
48 green buds (240)

Position ¼" smaller
petals and tack in plac

Then applique top peta
in place over first petal

Center Guide
for pink and
green petals

Quilt Setting Diagram for Country Rose

JACKIE'S TULIPS
Shown on page 35

Materials: 45-inch cotton or cotton blend fabrics in the following colors and amounts: 3 yards dark green, 1 yard light bright green, 1½ yards dark red, 7 yards wisteria, ½ yard yellow/red tiny print; quilting thread to match each fabric, four packages (3 yards each) wisteria or dark green 1-inch binding tape; king-size dacron batting (this will need about a 6-inch addition); king-size muslin sheet (hems opened and laundered) for lining; for ornamental stitching the following embroidery floss is needed: DMC No. 973 yellow, No. 498 red, No. 890 dark green and Susan Bates No. 0108 wisteria, No. 0132 bright blue, No. 0237 bright green; cardboard for templates, polyester stuffing to stuff tulip centers.

Quilt is approximately 96 x 99 inches.

Make cardboard templates using flower applique patterns. Mark around templates with pencil and add ¼-inch seams when cutting. Cut the following applique parts: Part A-8 pieces from dark red, Part B-74 pieces from dark red (set aside 56 for border applique), Part C-82 pieces from yellow/red print (set aside 56 for border applique), Part D-9 pieces from light bright green, Part D reversed-9 pieces from light bright green, Part E-8 pieces from dark green, Part E reversed-8 pieces from dark green, Part F-8 pieces from dark green.

To make center block, cut a 40 inch square from wisteria fabric (39 inches finished). Cut two strips 40 x 2½ inches (39 x 2 inches finished) from dark green. Sew to sides of wisteria block. Press seams toward green. Cut two strips 44 x 2½ inches (43 x 2 inches finished) and sew to bottom and top of wisteria block, including two

side green strips. Press toward green and trim evenly.

Arrange tulip applique parts as shown on diagram. Pin, baste and hand finish with blind-stitching. Before closing seam on yellow/red print centers, slip in small amount of stuffing, spread it around, then close seam. Anchor on back with long basting stitches.
See Diagram 1.

To make second section, cut two strips 44 x 16 inches (43 x 15½ inches finished) from wisteria. Sew these to sides of center block and press toward green. Cut two strips 75 x 16 inches (74½ x 15½ inches finished) from wisteria and sew to top and bottom of block including all side strips. Press toward green. Trim evenly.

Cut two strips 74 x 2½ inches

Diagram 1 of Center Block with tulip applique and green border.

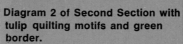

Diagram 2 of Second Section with tulip quilting motifs and green border.

Diagram 3 of Third Section (with tulip appliques; same tulip designs will be quilted between these parts), and green outside border.

Diagram 4

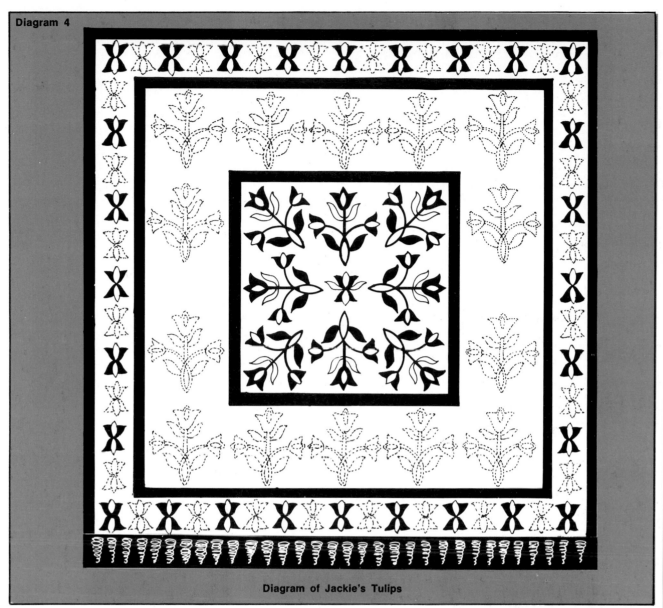

Diagram of Jackie's Tulips

(73½ x 2 inches finished) from dark green and sew to sides of wisteria. Press toward green. Cut two strips 78 x2½ inches (77½ x 2 inches finished) from dark green and sew to tops and bottom of block including two green strips. Press all seams toward green. Trim. See diagram 2.

To make third section, cut two strips 78 x 8 inches (77½ x 7½ inches finished) from wisteria for two more side strips. Press toward green. Cut two strips 92 x 8 inches (91½ x 7 inches finished) from wisteria and sew to top and bottom including side strips. Press and trim. See diagram 3.

To make outside border, cut two strips 92 x 2½ inches (91½ x 2 inches finished) from dark green. Sew on sides and press toward green. Cut one strip 96 x 2½ inches (95½ x 2 inches finished) from dark green and sew to top of quilt for border including two green **side strips. Cut one strip 96 x 8 inches** (95½ x 7½ inches finished) from dark green for bottom border strip. Press toward green and trim. If ornamental swirl stitching is used, this strip can be trimmed to 6 inches. If a continuation of quilting same as bottom row of quilt is used, then you will need the entire 8 inches. The ornamental stitching (to be done after work is complete) can be

drawn free-hand or use the quilting motif given. One strand is taken from each of the six colors of embroidery floss, put together in one needle and with quilt tight in hoop backstitch the swirl design, repeating it across the bottom border. If desired, the same combination of floss can be used on seam lines of wisteria fabric after first backstitching in green. See diagram 4.

To applique outside wisteria section, arrange tulip applique parts evenly around third section. See diagram 4. Pin, baste, blindstitch. Use same design for quilting in between these parts. See diagram 5.

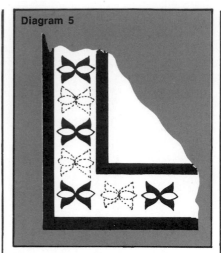

Diagram 5

Use entire tulip pattern for drawing quilting lines within the second section. Use diagram for a guide. All quilting motifs are outlines of the various appliques. See diagram 6.

Quilt in the ditch around appliques and along both sides of green strips. The following stitching is done last along with quilting after the center block is all quilted. Pull quilt up tight in hoop and backstitch entire tulip quilting motif in colors using two strands of embroidery floss. Use red for tulip blossom outlines, green for top leaves and dark blue for stems and bottom leaves.

Do border quilting as explained in outside border on page 149. instructions. See diagram 4.

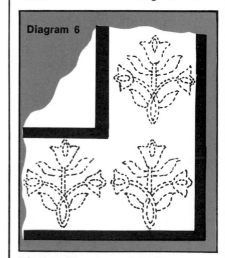

Diagram 6

Bind quilt using wisteria or dark green binding or in manner of your choice.

150

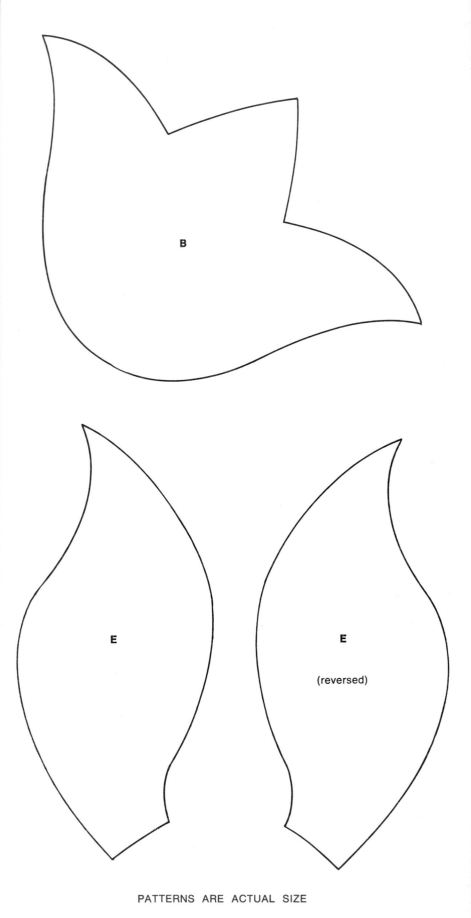

B

E

E

(reversed)

PATTERNS ARE ACTUAL SIZE

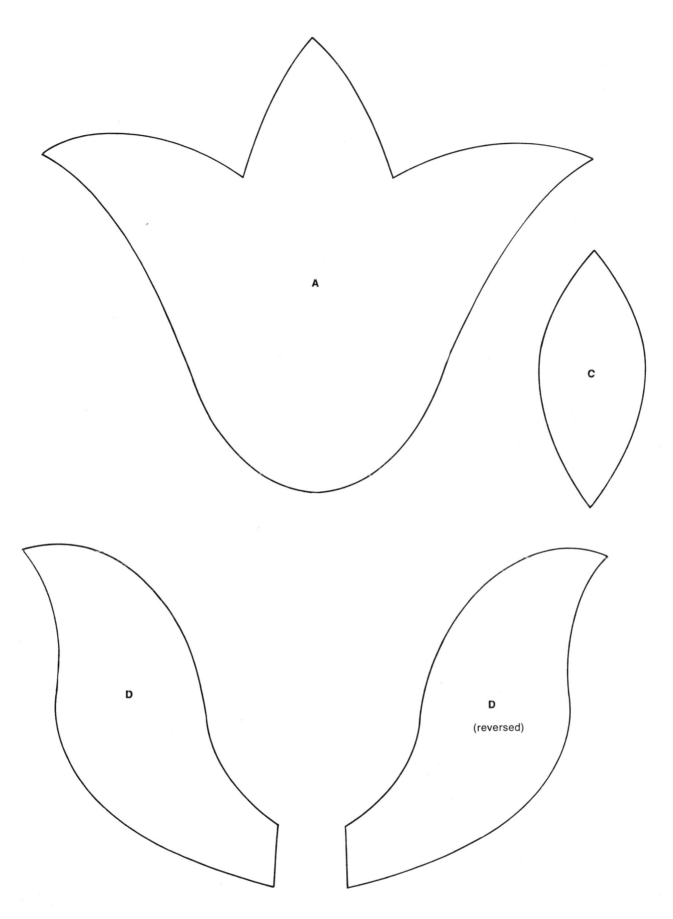

Add ¼-inch seam allowance when cutting fabric.

Connect A to A and B to B to form complete pattern

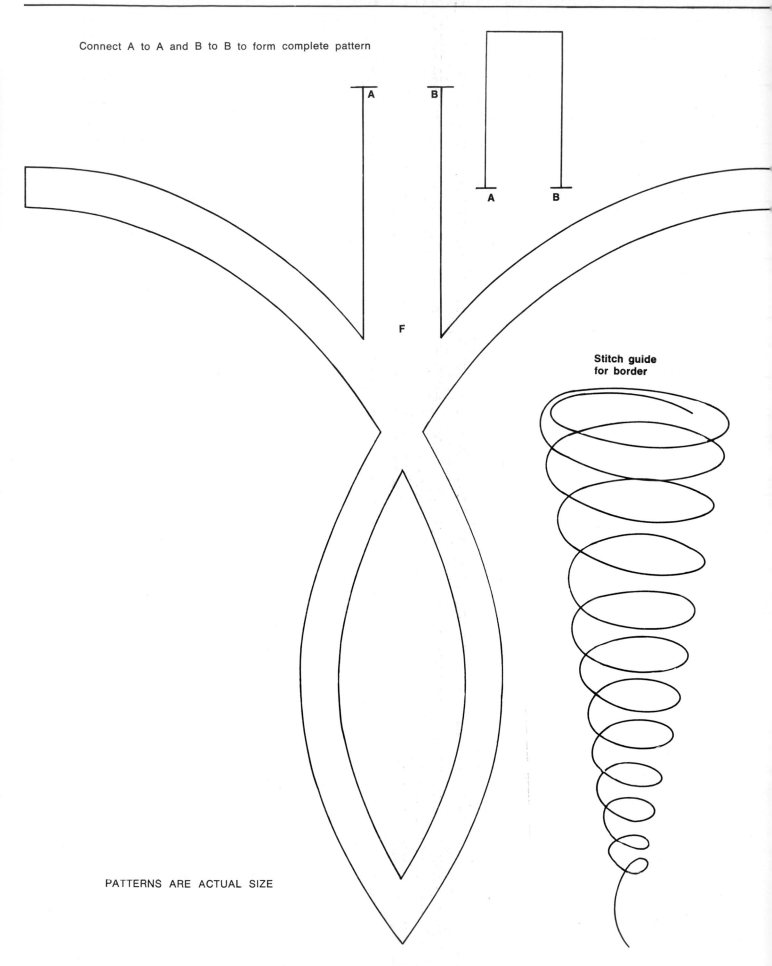

F

Stitch guide
for border

PATTERNS ARE ACTUAL SIZE

Diagram showing applique parts in position

EACH SQUARE EQUALS 1 INCH

153

JOANNE'S QUILT
Shown on page 39

Materials: 3⅛ yards dark blue calico (Color A), 5 yards yellow cotton or poly/cotton blend (Color B), 5½ yards any color of fabric for backing, ¾ yard yellow or any other color fabric for binding, polyester quilt batt, **quilting thread.**

Finished size of quilt: 80 x 80 inches.

This quilt is made by piecing 2-inch squares and 2-inch triangles together according to the piecing diagram below which constitutes one block. You will piece 18 of these blocks for the quilt. Each block requires eight squares of Color A, 24 triangles of Color A, 40 squares of Color B and 24 triangles of Color B. In all you will cut 144 squares of Color A and 432 triangles of Color A; 720 squares of Color B and 432 triangles of Color B.

Piece 18 blocks according to the diagram.

Join the finished blocks together in six rows of three blocks each.

To make border, cut two strips of Color A 4 x 72 inches and two strips of Color A 4 x 80 inches (finished measurements, add for seam allowances). These strips may be pieced if desired. Sew the shorter strips to the sides of the quilt. Sew the long strips across the top and bottom of the quilt.

To quilt, seam backing fabric to make an 80 x 80-inch square. Press seam allowances open. Lay the backing out on a flat surface, lay batting over backing, spread the quilt top over both and baste the three layers together for quilting in a frame or hoop. Quilt according to quilting diagram. All quilting lines are ¼ inch apart and ¼ inch from the seams. In the border, quilt parallel lines 1 inch apart (optional). See quilting diagram.

To bind the quilt, remove all basting threads. Trim lining and batting and quilt top even all around. Binding may be any width you desire. For a ½-inch binding allow ¼-inch seam allowance on either side of binding. Stitching through all three layers, sew one edge of binding to front of quilt all around. Turn binding over edge of quilt to back, fold binding seam allowance under and blindstitch to quilt backing.

PATTERNS ARE ACTUAL SIZE

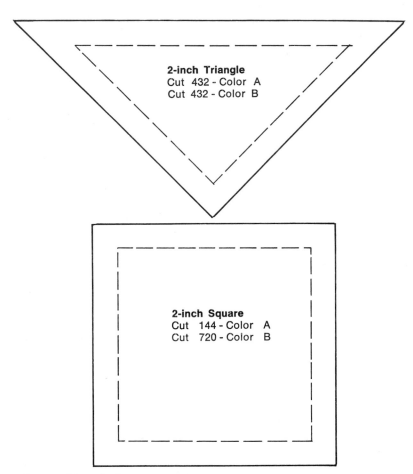

2-inch Triangle
Cut 432 - Color A
Cut 432 - Color B

2-inch Square
Cut 144 - Color A
Cut 720 - Color B

For machine piecing: Add seam allowances to all pieces when making templates. The pencil line will be your cutting line.
For hand piecing: Do not add seam allowances to pieces when making templates. Add seam allowance when cutting fabric. The pencil line will be your sewing line.

Piecing Diagram

Quilt setting for Joanne's Quilt

Quilting Diagram

VANISHING POINT
Shown on page 41

Materials: 45-inch cotton or cotton blend fabrics in the following colors and amounts (amounts are given in exact amounts, add extra for leeway and shrinkage): 2½ yards Color A-salmon, 2¾ yards Color B-light gray, 3⅛ yards Color C-navy (includes binding); polyester quilt batt; quilting thread to match fabrics; 6 yards of fabric of your choice for quilt lining.

Quilt is approximately 90 x 90 inches.

Note: Fabric amounts are exact (except for backing yardage), even using 44-inch fabric will make a great change. The yardages were figured for cutting the strips across the fabric, then piecing to make the length of the strips. With this method there is absolutely no waste, but there are extra seams.

Make templates of square and triangle pattern pieces. Using Quilt Diagram A make one, using squares, triangles and

3-inch strips as indicated. Total pieces for this section are charted below (measurements are finished sizes):

Begin with four rectangles at the top center. Add a row on each side, then a row at the bottom. Continue in this fashion until this part of quilt is complete. Asterisks on Quilt Diagram A indicate where two or three rows are added on the bottom so the side strips will fit.

Using Quilt Diagram B make one, again using squares,

Quilt Diagram A - Make 1

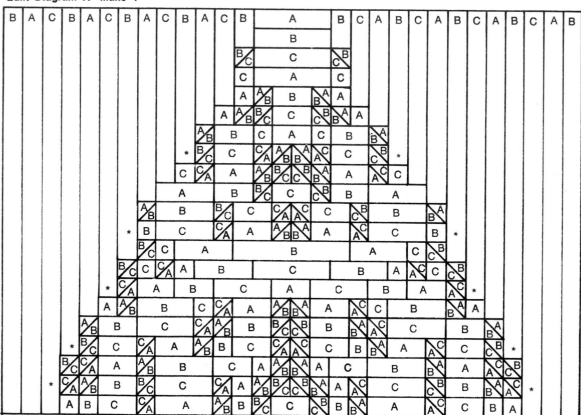

Total pieces required for this section—finished measurements.

Color A	Color B	Color C
14 sq.	8 sq.	12 sq.
62 tri.	62 tri.	56 tri.
14-3 x 6″ strips	15-3 x 6″ strips	15-3 x 6″ strips
6-3 x 9″ strips	8-3 x 9″ strips	8-3 x 9″ strips
2-3 x 12″ strips	1-3 x 12″ strip	2-3 x 12″ strips
2-3 x 18″ strips	1-3 x 18″ strip	2-3 x 15″ strips
2-3 x 30″ strips	2-3 x 24″ strips	2-3 x 27″ strips
2-3 x 48″ strips	2-3 x 39″ strips	2-3 x 45″ strips
2-3 x 63″ strips	2-3 x 54″ strips	2-3 x 63″ strips
	2-3 x 63″ strips	

156

triangles and 3-inch strips as indicated. Total pieces for this section are as charted below (measurements are finished sizes).
Arrows on Quilt Diagram B show where to divide the section for easier piecing. Piece each section in rows, then join.
Join the two quilt sections (A and B) to form quilt top.

Sandwich quilt lining fabric, quilt batt and quilt top and quilt each strip ¼ inch from seam using thread to match fabric.
Bind with navy fabric.

Quilt Diagram B - Make 1

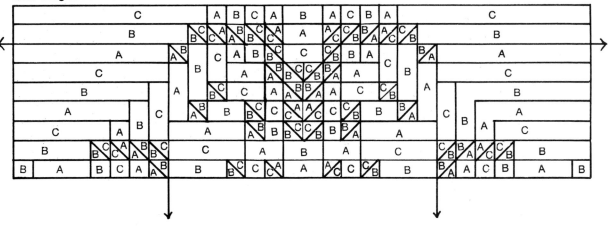

Total pieces required for this section—finished measurements.

Color A	Color B	Color C
12 sq.	10 sq.	8 sq.
26 tri.	36 tri.	30 tri.
6-3 x 6″ strips	6-3 x 6″ strips	5-3 x 6″ strips
4-3 x 9″ strips	4-3 x 9″ strips	2-3 x 9″ strips
2-3 x 12″ strips	2-3 x 12″ strips	2-3 x 12″ strips
2-3 x 18″ strips	2-3 x 21″ strips	2-3 x 15″ strips
2-3 x 24″ strips	2-3 x 27″ strips	2-3 x 24″ strips
		2-3 x 30″ strips

PATTERNS ARE ACTUAL SIZE

For machine piecing: Add seam allowances to all pieces when making templates. The pencil line will be your cutting line. **For hand piecing:** Do not add seam allowances to pieces when making templates. Add seam allowance when cutting fabric. The pencil line will be your sewing line.

EVOLUTION
Shown on page 43

Materials: 45-inch cotton or cotton blend fabrics in the following colors and amounts (amounts are given in exact inches, add extra for leeway and shrinkage): 87½ inches Color A-light green, 56 inches Color B-dark green, 49 inches Color C-dark brown, 40 inches Color D-tan, 78 inches Color E-white; 20 inches additional dark green fabric for binding; 6 yards of fabric of your choice for quilt lining; polyester quilt batting; quilting thread in colors to match fabrics.

Quilt is approximately 90 x 90 inches.

Note: Fabric amounts are exact, even using 44-inch fabric will make a great change.
Make templates of all quilt pattern pieces and make twenty of quilt block A.

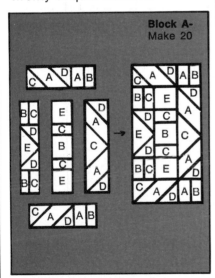

Block A-
Make 20

Total pieces required for making all twenty of Block A:

Color A	Color B	Color C
80 rhom.	20 sq.	40 tri.
40 rect.	80 rect.	20 tri.-2
		80 rect.

Color D	Color E
120 tri.	40 sq.
	20-tri.-2

When you have pieced all twenty blocks, make two rows of ten blocks each. These are the top two rows of the quilt. See photograph for placement.
Make five of block B.

Total pieces required for making all five of block B:

Color A	Color B	Color C
40 rhom.	20 sq.	20 tri.
20 rect.	20 rect.	

Color D	Color E
40 tri.	20 sq.
	30 tri.-2
	40 rect.

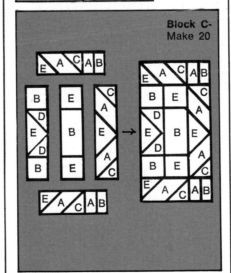

Block C-
Make 20

When you have pieced all five blocks, join them to form the center strip of the quilt. Make sure to have them right side up.
Make 20 of block C.
Total pieces required for

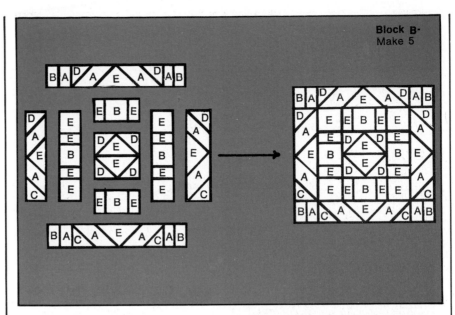

Block B-
Make 5

making all twenty of block C:

Color A	Color B	Color C
80 rhom.	40 rect.	80 tri.
40 rect.	40 sq.	
	20 rect.-2	

Color D	Color E
40 tri.	40 tri.-2
	40 sq.
	40 tri.

When you have pieced all twenty blocks, join them in two rows of ten each. These are the bottom two rows of the quilt. See photograph for placement.
The following chart is the amounts you will cut of each color and shape for the entire quilt top:

Color A	Color B	Color C
200 rhom.	80 sq.	140 tri.
100 rect.	140 rect.	20 tri.-2
	20 rect.-2	80 rect.

Color D	Color E
200 tri.	100 sq.
	40 tri.
	90 tri.-2
	40 rect.

When you have pieced and joined all blocks baste quilt top, quilt batting and lining together and outline-quilt each piece ¼-inch in from seam areas using quilt thread to match fabrics. Quilt a cross in all white diamond areas.
Bind quilt using dark green yardage.

159

Make templates for Evolution—add seam allowance when cutting fabric.

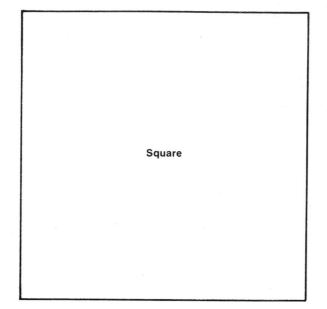

Square

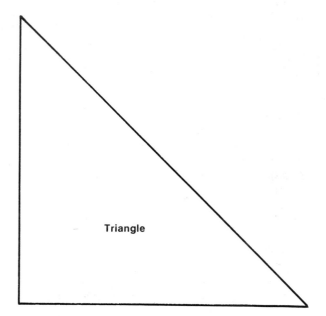

Triangle

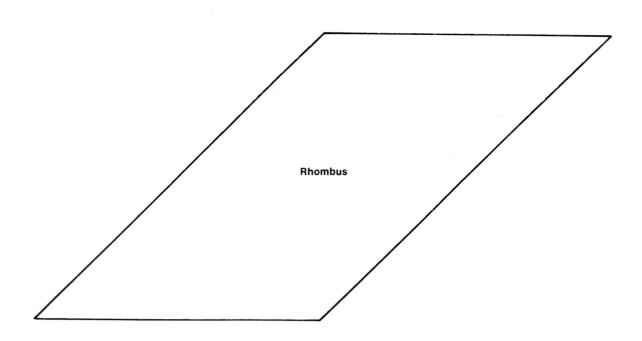

Rhombus

PATTERNS ARE ACTUAL SIZE

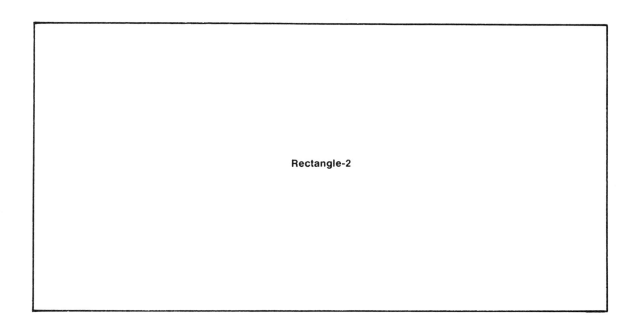

Rectangle-2

For machine piecing: Add seam allowances to all pieces when making templates. The pencil line will be your cutting line.
For hand piecing: Do not add seam allowances to pieces when making templates. Add seam allowance when cutting fabric. The pencil line will be your sewing line.

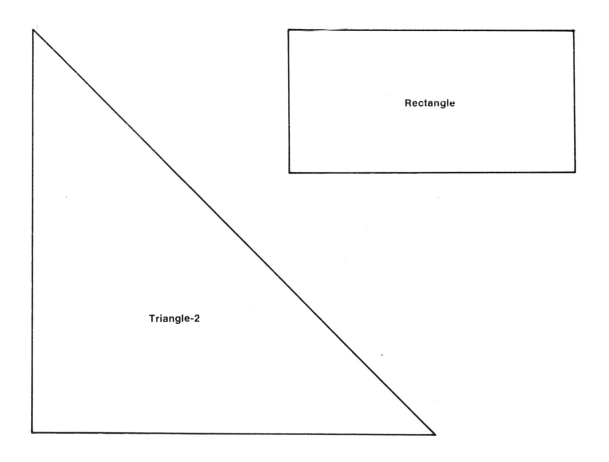

Rectangle

Triangle-2

dark brown

dark green

light green

tan

SWEET DREAMS
Shown on page 45

Materials: Cotton or cotton blend fabric in the following colors and amounts (amounts are exact in inches for 45-inch fabric, add extra for leeway and shrinkage). Cutting scheme calls for 22 triangles each row across fabric and 12 squares each row across fabric: 88 inches of Color A-gold, 56 inches of Color B-yellow check or print, 88 inches of Color C-green, 101 inches of Color D-white, 20 inches of any color (gold used on quilt shown) for binding, polyester quilt batting, quilting thread to match each color of fabric, lining fabric in color of your choice (6 yds.).

Quilt is approximately 90 x 90 inches.

This quilt is made up of six rows of six blocks each for a total of 36 blocks. Each of the 36 blocks requires 13 triangles of Color A, 8 triangles of Color B, 13 triangles of Color C, 2 squares of Color D and 12 triangles of Color D. Make templates of square and triangles. Piece each block according to the diagarm below. Each block composed of five pieced strips. Strips are stitched together to form a square.

You will cut a total of 468 triangles of Color A, 288 triangles of Color B, 468 triangles of Color C, 72 squares of Color D and 432 triangles of Color D.

Join the blocks into six rows of six blocks each. Make sure they are right side up by checking photograph if necessary.

Sandwich the quilt lining, polyester batting and quilt top and quilt according to diagram below. All outline quilting is ¼ inch from seam. Quilting in white (Color D) areas begins ¼ inch from seams and is ¾ inch apart.

Bind quilt in color of your choice.

Piecing Diagram

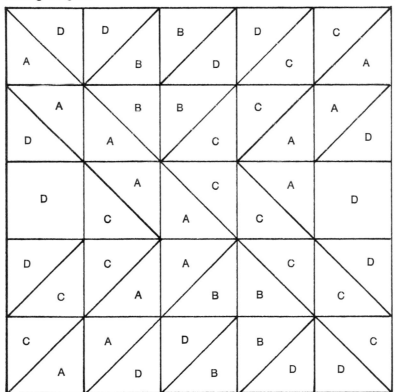

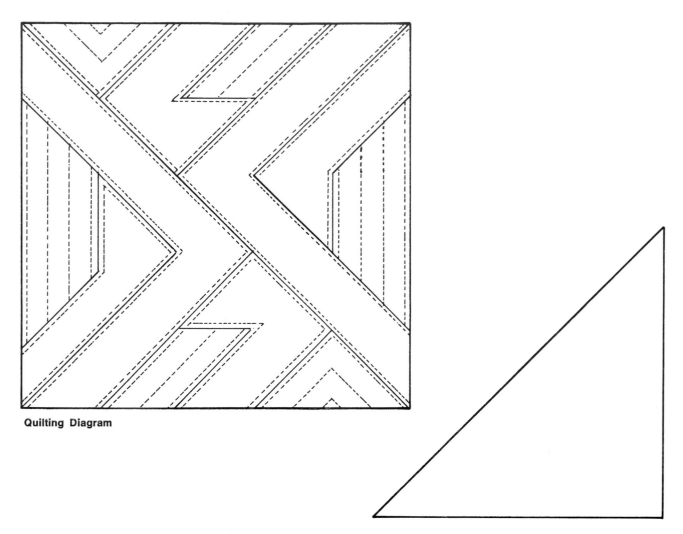

Quilting Diagram

For machine piecing: Add seam allowances to all pieces when making templates. The pencil line will be your cutting line.
For hand piecing: Do not add seam allowances to pieces when making templates. Add seam allowance when cutting fabric. The pencil line will be your sewing line.

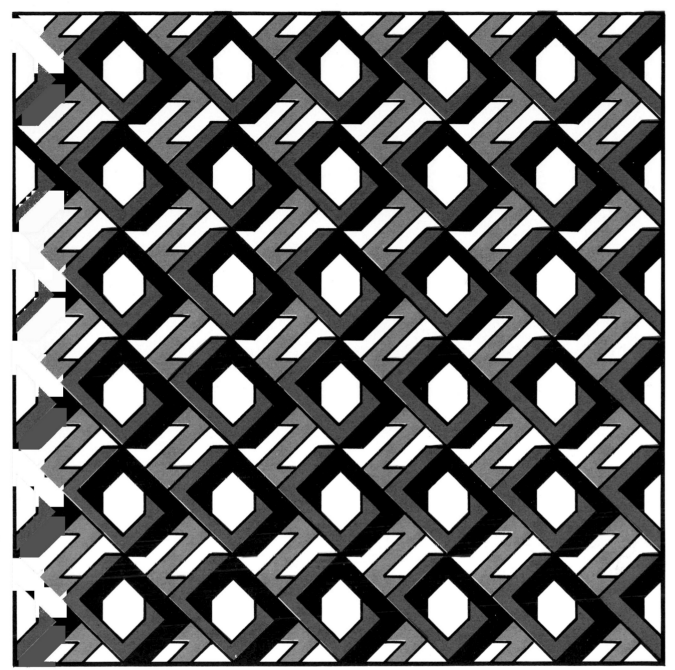

Quilt Setting for Sweet Dreams

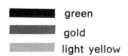 green

gold

light yellow

HOLY MAN
Shown on page 47

Materials: 45-inch cotton or cotton blend fabrics in the following colors and amounts (amounts are given in exact amounts, add extra for leeway and shrinkage): 3¼ yards of Color A-salmon, 3¼ yards of Color B-turquoise, 4¼ yards of Color C-white (includes fabric for binding) (lining will have to be pieced from 7½ yards of fabric); polyester batting; quilting thread to match fabric colors.

Quilt is approximately 96 x 96 inches.

Note: Fabric amounts are exact, even using 44-inch fabric will make a change, except for backing yardage.

Make templates of all quilt pattern pieces. Add seam allowances to templates only if you are machine piecing.

Piece sixteen quilt blocks according to the diagram. Each block is pieced in nine strips running from top to bottom and then the nine strips are stitched together to make the block.

Total pieces required for making all sixteen blocks:

Color A	Color B	Color C
32 sq.	32 sq.	64 sq.
192 tri.	192 tri.	128 tri.
96 **rect.**	96 **rect.**	128 **rect.**

After all sixteen blocks are pieced, set blocks together in four rows of four blocks each making sure to keep blocks right side up when joining.

Baste finished quilt top, quilt batting and lining together and quilt each block according to the quilting diagram.

After quilting is complete, bind the quilt using white yardage.

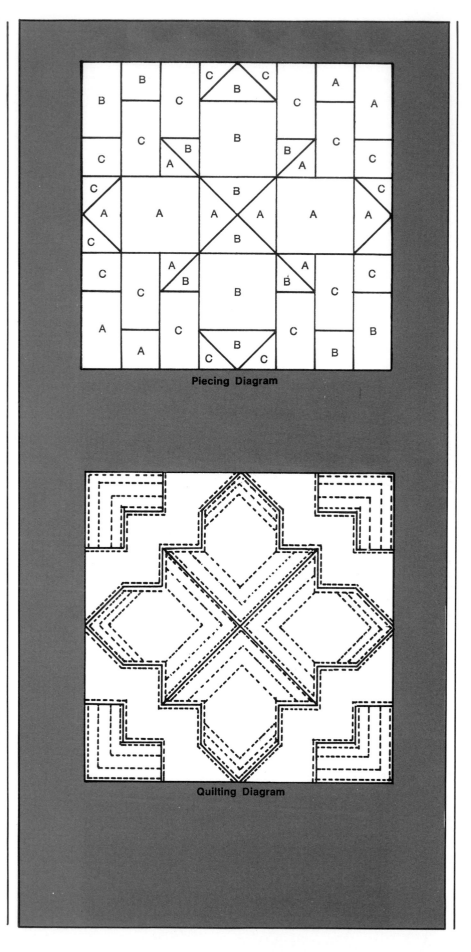

Piecing Diagram

Quilting Diagram

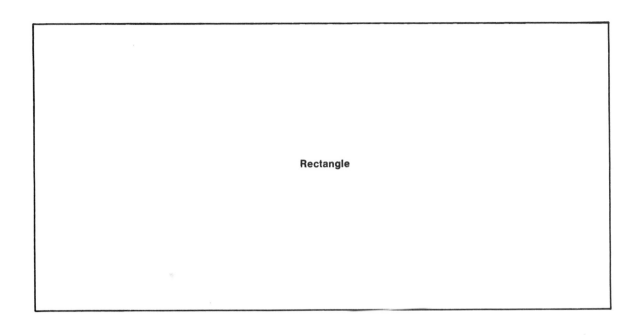

Rectangle

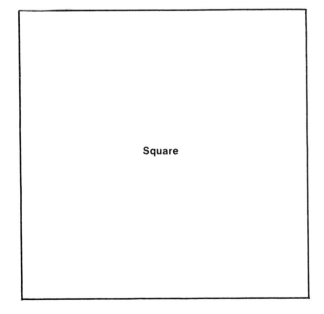

Square

For machine piecing: Add seam allowances to all pieces when making templates. The pencil line will be your cutting line.
For hand piecing: Do not add seam allowances to pieces when making templates. Add seam allowance when cutting fabric. The pencil line will be your sewing line.

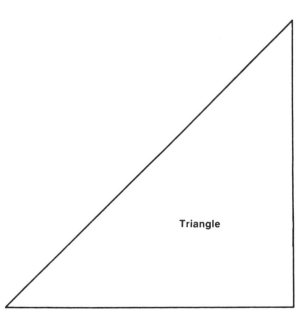

Triangle

PATTERNS ARE ACTUAL SIZE

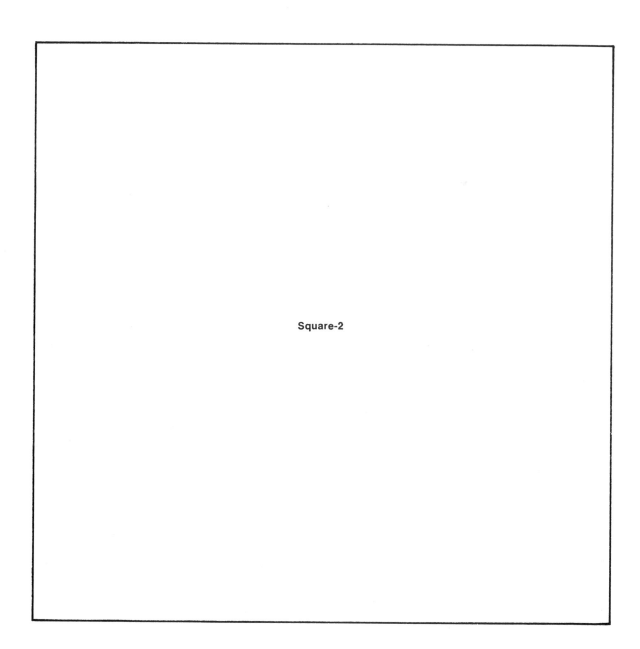

Square-2

For machine piecing: Add seam allowances to all pieces when making templates. The pencil line will be your cutting line.
For hand piecing: Do not add seam allowances to pieces when making templates. Add seam allowance when cutting fabric. The pencil line will be your sewing line.

Triangle-2

Quilt Setting for Holy Man

SYMPHONY IN F
Shown on page 49

Materials: 45-inch fabric in the following colors and amounts: 190 inches (5¾ yards) color a-white; 87 inches (2¾ yards) color b-blue; 8 inches (⅜ yard) color c-yellow; ¾ yard binding fabric in matching or contrasting color; 6 yards backing fabric in any color; 90 x 90-inches quilt batting and quilting threads.

Finished size: 90 x 90 inches.

Make templates of pattern pieces and cut the following pieces: color a (white) — 196 squares, 252 triangles; b (blue) — 36 squares, 216 triangles; color c (yellow) — 36 triangles.

Add seam allowances and cut the following pieces (no pattern provided): From white — 8 large rectangles (6 x 12 inches), 4 center rectangles (6 x 3 inches), 4 small rectangles (6 x 9 inches), two strips (cut across the fabric and piece) 6 x 72 inches, four strips (cut across the fabric and piece) 3 x 72 inches. From blue — two strips (cut across the fabric and piece) 3 x 48 inches, two strips (cut across the fabric and piece) 3 x 72 inches.

Note that you are working with two "F" blocks that are mirrors of each other. Refer to the piecing diagram when you begin to join them into strips so each block will be going in the right direction. The "F" design is contained in Blocks A and B, which have the same number of pieces with the "F" reversed. For each Block A and Block B, use 7 squares color a-white, 8 triangles color a-white, 1 square color b-blue, 8 triangles color b-blue. Make 12 Block A and 12 Block B.

Each Block C requires 3 triangles a-white, 3 triangles c-yellow, 1 square a-white. Make four Block C's.

Each Block D requires 6 triangles a-white, 6 triangles c-yellow, 2 squares a-white. Make four Block D's.

Each Block E requires 3 squares b-blue, 4 squares a-white, 2 triangles b-blue, 2 triangles a-white. Make two Block E's. Block F uses identical pieces to those of Block E, but their placement is reversed (see piecing diagram). Make two Block F's.

Construct a center block using four 3 x 6-inch Center Rectangles, 16 triangles color a-white and 16 triangles color b-blue.

Work from center block out, first joining Large Rectangles to either side of center block. Make two strips composed of one Block A and one Block B with a lengthwise Large

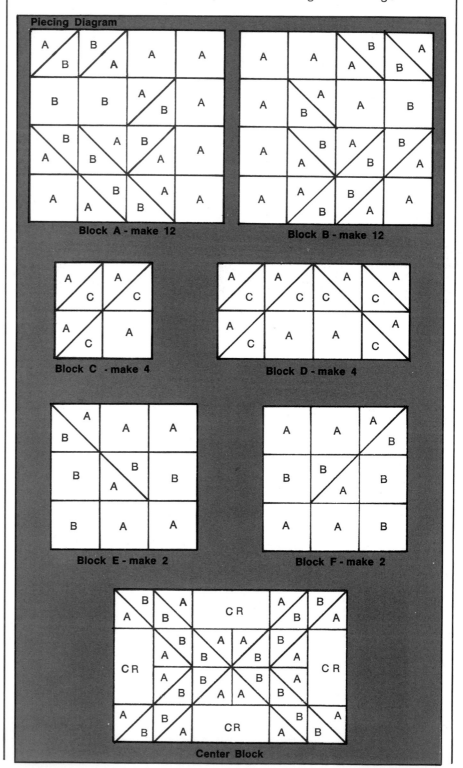

Piecing Diagram

Block A - make 12

Block B - make 12

Block C - make 4

Block D - make 4

Block E - make 2

Block F - make 2

Center Block

Rectangle between A and B; join these strips to the top and bottom of the center block as shown on piecing diagram.

Using Blocks C and D and Large and Small Rectangles, make strips of blocks as shown in the illustration below. Join short strips to top and bottom of work. Join a long strip to each side.

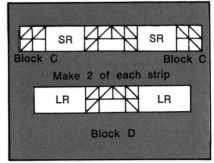

Join two 3 x 48-inch (plus seam allowance) strips in color b-blue to sides of work. Place Blocks A and B around outside of work as shown in piecing diagram, starting with Block A in upper left corner and Block B in lower left corner and placing blocks as shown. First construct long strips of Blocks A and B, then attach to work in strips.

Construct two strips, each composed of one 6 x 72-inch (plus seam allowance) strip in color a-white and 3 x 72-inch (plus seam allowance) strip in color b-blue. Join each strip to sides of work with b-blue strips to outside of work.

Construct two strips, each composed of two 3 x 72-inch (plus seam allowance) strips in color a-white and one 3 x 72-inch (plus seam allowance) strip in color b-blue; the blue strip will be between the two white strips, as shown in piecing diagram. Join a Block E to left end of strip and a Block F to right end of strip. Sew one entire strip across top of quilt. Turn other entire strip upside down and sew across bottom of quilt. See piecing diagram for placement before sewing. Join one pieced strip to top of work and one pieced strip to bottom.

Form a sandwich of the quilt top, batting, and quilt backing fabric. Smooth wrinkles and baste through all three layers to hold in place while quilting. **Quilt** through all layers of fabric in accordance with quilting diagrams. For Blocks A and B, see Diagram 1. For Block C, see Diagram 2. For center section, see Diagram 3. For Small Rectangle, see Diagram 4. For Large Rectangle, see Diagram 5; quilt the pattern of Diagram 5 in the 6-inch color a-white areas of the border; the pattern will repeat exactly six times on either side (on each strip). On top and bottom border sections, quilt ¼ inch from seam line.

To bind the quilt, remove all basting threads. Trim lining and batting and quilt top evenly all around. Binding may be any width desired. For a ½-inch binding, allow ¼-inch seam allowance on either side of binding. Stitching through all three layers, sew one edge of binding to front of quilt all around. Turn binding over edge of quilt to back, fold binding seam allowance under, and blindstitch to quilt backing.

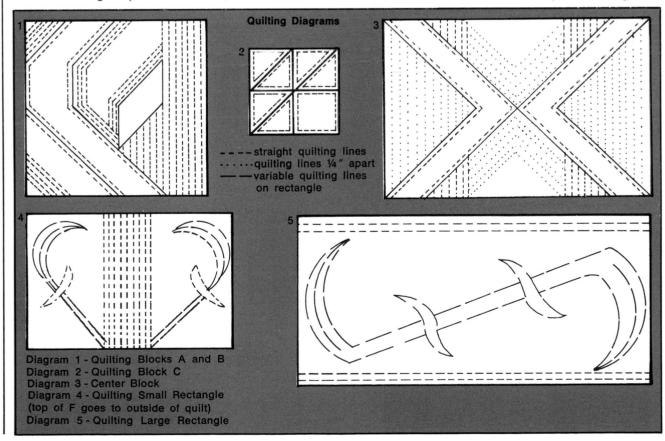

Diagram 1 - Quilting Blocks A and B
Diagram 2 - Quilting Block C
Diagram 3 - Center Block
Diagram 4 - Quilting Small Rectangle
(top of F goes to outside of quilt)
Diagram 5 - Quilting Large Rectangle

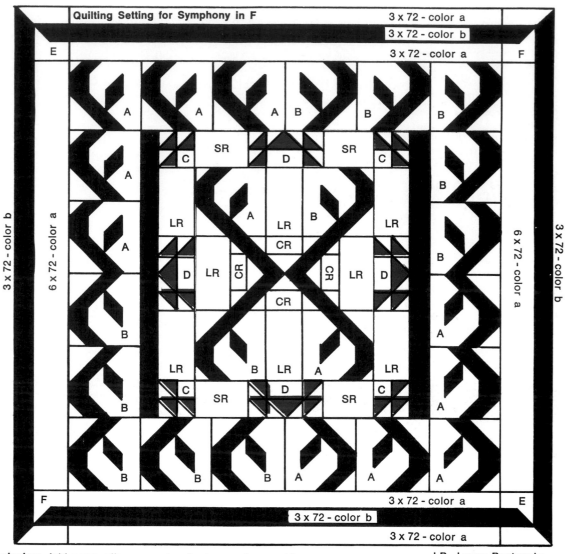

Quilting Setting for Symphony in F

3 x 72 - color a
3 x 72 - color b
3 x 72 - color a

E · F

3 x 72 - color b · 6 x 72 - color a

6 x 72 - color a · 3 x 72 - color b

F · E

3 x 72 - color a
3 x 72 - color b
3 x 72 - color a

For machine piecing: Add seam allowances to all pieces when making templates. The pencil line will be your cutting line.

For hand piecing: Do not add seam allowances to pieces when making templates. Add seam allowance when cutting fabric. The pencil line will be your sewing line.

LR - Large Rectangle
SR - Small Rectangle
CR - Center Rectangle

PATTERNS ARE ACTUAL SIZE

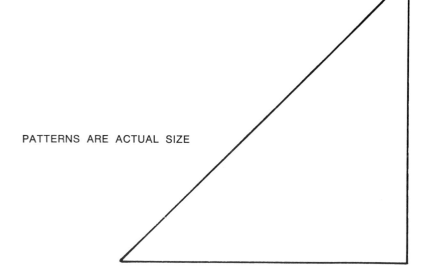

172

ORIENTAL BLOSSOM
Shown on page 53

Materials: Dark blue embroidery floss; 6 yards dark blue fabric; ½ yard medium blue fabric; 1½ yards light blue fabric; 7¼ yards white fabric; light blue fabric for backing (or use a sheet); polyester quilt batt; yardage for ¾-inch light blue bias strips for Chinese characters; yardage for ¾-inch dark blue bias strips for flower stems and Chinese characters; yardage for 3-inch navy bias binding for binding quilt.

Finished size of quilt is 92 x 108 inches.

Using quilt setting diagram cut all background fabrics first, starting with longest piece. Note that all measurements are finished measurements and be sure to add seam allowances. Cut two pieces 10 x 98 inches from white fabric, one piece 10 x 92 inches from white fabric, two pieces 15 x 92 inches from white fabric, one piece 21 x 36 inches from white fabric, one piece 13 x 36 inches from white fabric, two pieces 26 x 30 inches from white fabric, two pieces 3 x 72 inches from dark blue fabric, two pieces 3 x 92 inches from dark blue fabric, two pieces 3 x 58 inches from dark blue fabric, two pieces 3 x 30 inches from dark blue fabric.

Applique flower designs to the two 26 x 30 white rectangles before assembling pieces of quilt. Use the pattern given for flower design four times on each piece. This design is for the upper right hand side of the fabric, reverse for left side, turn upside down for lower right side and turn upside down in reverse for lower left side. The butterfly only appears in the upper right of the top piece of fabric and upper left of the lower piece of fabric. The stems of the flowers are ¾-inch dark blue bias strips

folded in ¼ inch on each side. See illustration below for flower arrangement of top piece of fabric, duplicate arrangement in second piece of fabric except for butterfly placement.

Next, enlarge Chinese characters and applique bias-strip characters to the proper pieces of white fabric. The characters are formed by pressing dark blue bias strips so raw edges are in center of tape, fold in ¼ inch on raw edge of light blue tape and baste to right side of dark blue tape. You now have a ½ inch tape which will be used for most of the characters. There are some small pieces of dark blue tape that are made by turning in both sides of the dark blue tape.

The characters (1-6) on the right hand white fabric panel are placed approximately as follows: top of the first character is 1½ inches from top edge (none of the measurements include seam allowance, but are finished measurements) in a 14¾ inch space, next allow 5 inches for quilted key design (all quilting is done after quilt is assembled), the next character is in an 11-inch space, then allow 5 inches for quilted key design, the next character is centered in an 8½ inch space, then allow 5 inches for quilted key design, next character is in an 8½ inch space, allow 5 inches for quilted key design, next character is in an 8½ inch

space, allow 5 inches for key design. The final character on the right hand side is in a 14½ inch space with bottom of design being 7 inches from bottom edge of panel. Characters 1-6 read "enjoy one's life."

The characters (7-12) on the left hand white fabric panel are placed in the same positions so that they fall approximately opposite the characters on the right hand side. Characters 7-12 read "a beautiful and lovely individual."

Characters in top panel (13-14) are centered with space allowed for the quilted key design to be repeated under them and lining up with applique keys on right and left side panels. The characters in the bottom panel (15-16) are centered in the panel both horizontally and vertically. In both upper and lower panels the circle quilting design will be quilted at each end, slightly overlapping the seam between the side panels and the top and bottom panels and the temple design is quilted in between the two characters of both top and bottom panels, so allow for these quilting motifs as you place your characters. Characters 13-14 read "love, prosperity" and 15-16 read "happiness, long life."

Next, applique key design onto two outside white panels and bottom white panel. There are six key appliques on each side and across bottom, spaced approximately 1¾ inches apart, centered in the panels. In between first key designs at the top edge of quilt and second key design is a space for a quilted key, allow space for this quilt motif when positioning appliqued keys. Key is cut on the straight of the dark blue fabric. Cut strips 1½ inches wide, turn sides ¼ inch and baste, mitering corners, turn in ends. Use key motif pattern as a guide for constructing appliques. Baste in place on background fabric and applique.

Assemble all pieces of quilt as indicated on the quilt setting diagram. Make a sandwich of backing fabric, quilt batt and quilt top and baste.

After quilt is assembled draw quilt motifs in place: the key designs in between each character, the circle designs top and bottom, the temple designs in between the characters top and bottom, the key designs that fall after the first appliqued keys on each of the outside panels, the key designs under the characters on the top panel, a temple design in the center of each flower and a circle design centered on the seam between the two flower panels. Quilt in the ditch around all blue borders and appliques. Bind with navy binding.

Quilt setting for Oriental Blossom—add seam allowances to all measurements.

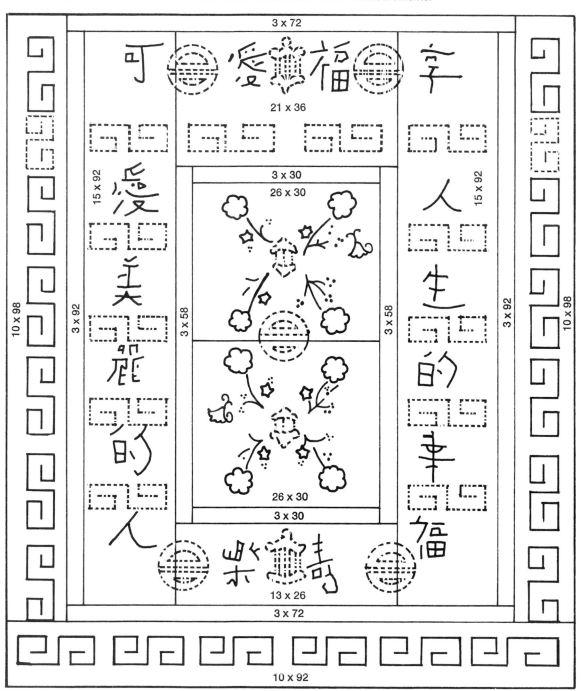

174

PATTERNS ARE ACTUAL SIZE

Dk. blue

Dk. blue embroidery

Dk. blue bias tape folded

Lt. blue

Lt. blue

Med. blue

Med. blue

Lt. blue

Dk. blue embroidery

Dk. blue

Dk. blue

Lt. blue

Lt. blue

Med. blue

Dk. blue embroidery

Dk. blue

Lt. blue

Dk. blue embroidery

Med. blue

Med. blue
blue

Med. blue
blue

Lt. blue

Dk. blue

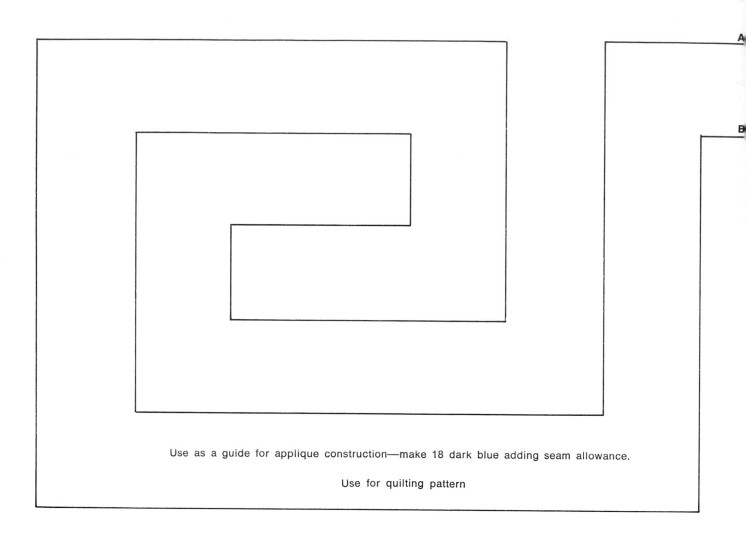

Use as a guide for applique construction—make 18 dark blue adding seam allowance.

Use for quilting pattern

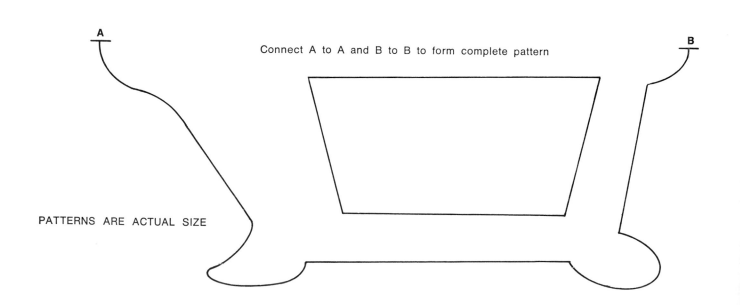

Connect A to A and B to B to form complete pattern

PATTERNS ARE ACTUAL SIZE

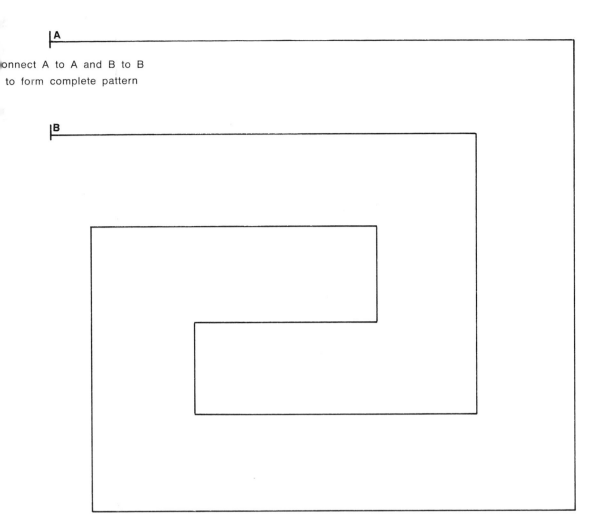

Connect A to A and B to B
to form complete pattern

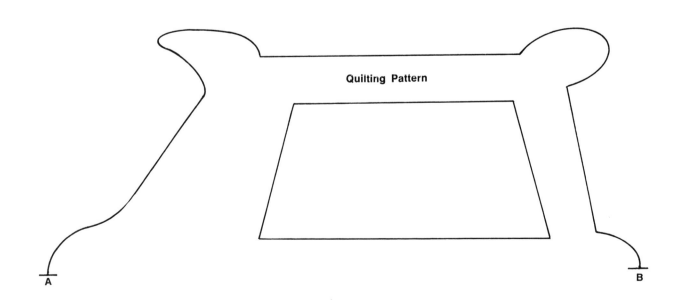

Quilting Pattern

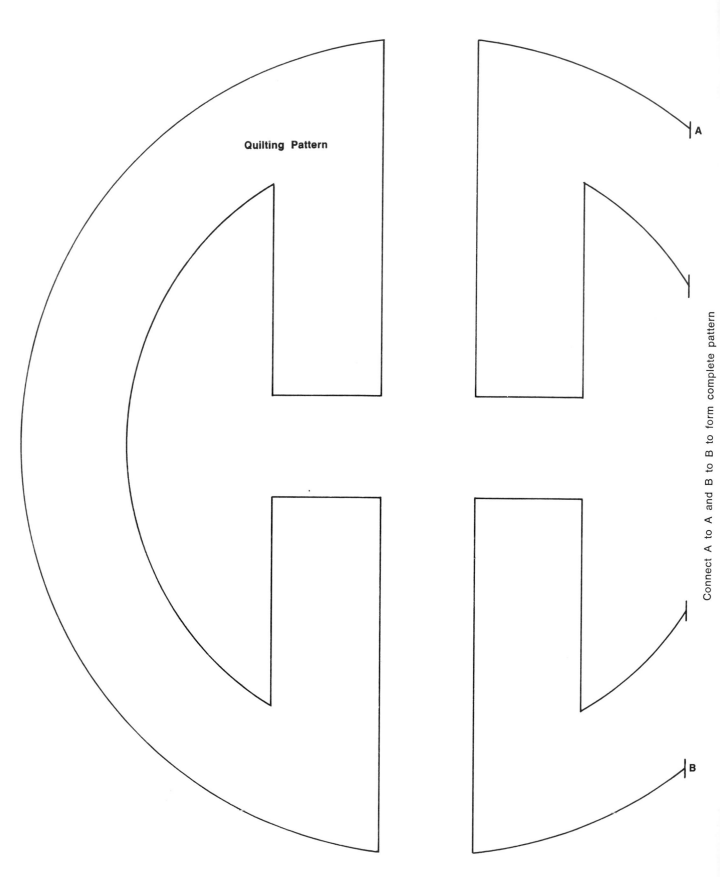

Quilting Pattern

A

Connect A to A and B to B to form complete pattern

B

PATTERNS ARE ACTUAL SIZE

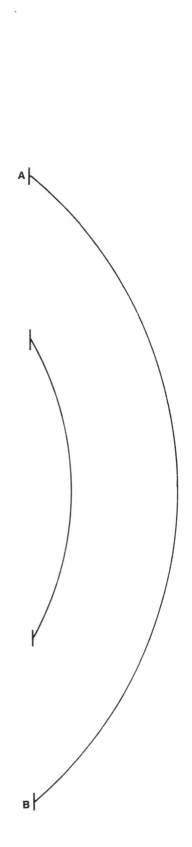

A

B

Dk. blue———

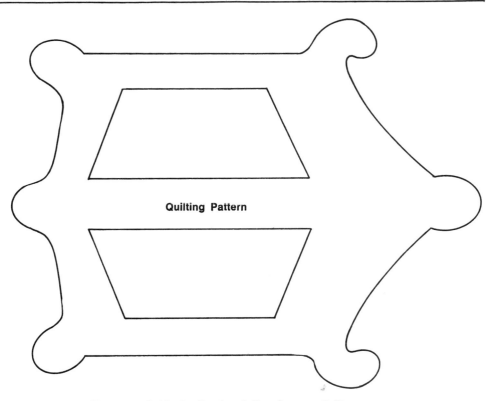

Quilting Pattern

Chinese Character Guide to Freehand Drawing on Quilt.

Note: Characters 1-6 are placed top to bottom down right side of quilt. 7-12 are placed top to bottom down left side of quilt. 13-14 are placed in the center top of quilt and 15-16 are placed in the center bottom of quilt.

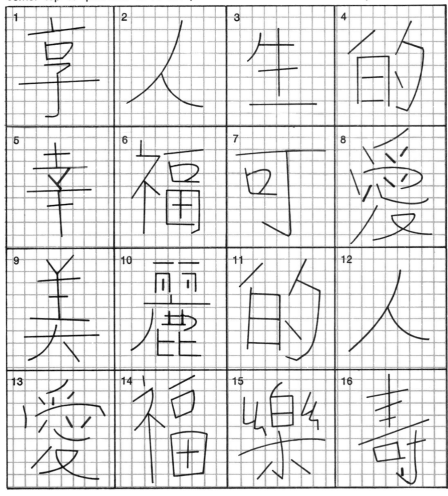

PEACH BLOSSOM
Shown on page 55

Materials: 10¼ yards pale peach cotton or cotton blend fabric for quilt top, applique and binding (for binding use either peach fabric or seam binding); 9 yards white fabric for lining, 1½ yards brown cotton or cotton blend for strips and bias stems (or use seam binding for stems); 1¼ yards peach print for flower petals; 1½ yards brown print for flower petals, 1¼ yards dark peach fabric for flower petals; 9 yards bonded batting; quilting thread to match pale peach fabric.

Quilt is approximately 108 x 110 inches and fits a king-size bed.

Refer to quilt diagram to see how quilt is constructed before beginning. The major elements of the quilt top are two 33 x 108-inch (add seam allowances) side panels of pale peach fabric, two 3 x 108-inch (add seam allowances) strips and one 38½ x 108-inch (add seam allowances) center panel. Six flowers are appliqued vertically down each side panel. Diagonal and horizontal quilting is done on each side panel with vertical quilt lines at the bottom outside corners of each panel which is cut on a curve. "Curve around two straight lines" motif is quilted the length of each 3-inch strip and center panel is quilted in repeating motifs of "flower with stems" and "corsage with a leaf" motif quilted on outside edge of center panel with each corsage motif.

Cut two side panels 38 x 108 inches (add seam allowances to all measurements and all applique pieces) from pale peach fabric. Curve the outside bottom corner on each panel as indicated on quilt diagram. Mark all quiting lines on each panel as indicated on quilt diagram. Diagonal lines are placed from inside edge of panel over 7½ inches. Then horizontal lines 2 inches apart are drawn to outside edge of quilt. (After applique work is done you will also quilt a straight line dividing the diagonal quilting from the horizontal from the top of the first flower to the top of the quilt.) 12 inches from the bottom of the quilt, change horizontal lines to vertical and horizontal "corners" as shown in quilt diagram.

Cut out all flower petal layers, centers, leaves and stems

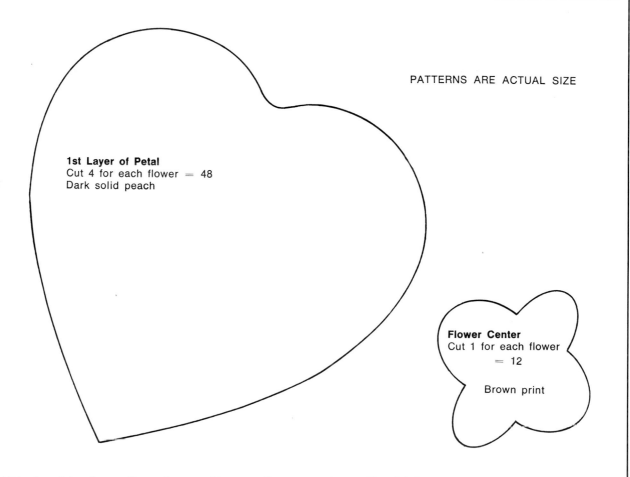

PATTERNS ARE ACTUAL SIZE

1st Layer of Petal
Cut 4 for each flower = 48
Dark solid peach

Flower Center
Cut 1 for each flower
= 12

Brown print

Make templates for applique pieces; add seam allowances when cutting fabric.

(stems are ½ inch finished strips cut on the bias or use bias tape).

Carefully baste stems, first petal layer and leaves in place as shown on quilt diagram. Tip of top flower is about 14 inches from top of quilt. Then flowers are placed on 16-inch centers (16 inches from center of first flower to center of second flower, etc.). Each flower consists of four of each of the four petal layers and are appliqued on top of each other with flower center appliqued on top of all four layers. There are 12 flowers in all, six on each side panel, so you will have 48 first layer petals, 48 second layer petals, 48 third layer petals, 48 fourth layer petals, 12 centers, 24 leaves plus ½ inch wide stems to go from flower to flower. Stems should be caught under first petal layer of each flower to conceal raw edges.

Applique all stems, leaves and flower petal layers and flower centers in place.

Cut two strips 3 x 108 inches from brown fabric and mark "curves around two straight lines" quilt motif down length of each strip. Cut center panel 38½ x 108 inches from pale peach fabric and mark quilting motifs as indicated on quilt diagram: "flower and stem" motif down center of panel, corsage motif on each side of panel with leaf design in place on outside of each corsage motif.

Join the side panels, brown strips and center panel. Quilt all quilting lines using thread to match pale peach fabric. Quilt in the ditch around stems, each petal layer on flowers and flower centers. Bind quilt with pale peach binding.

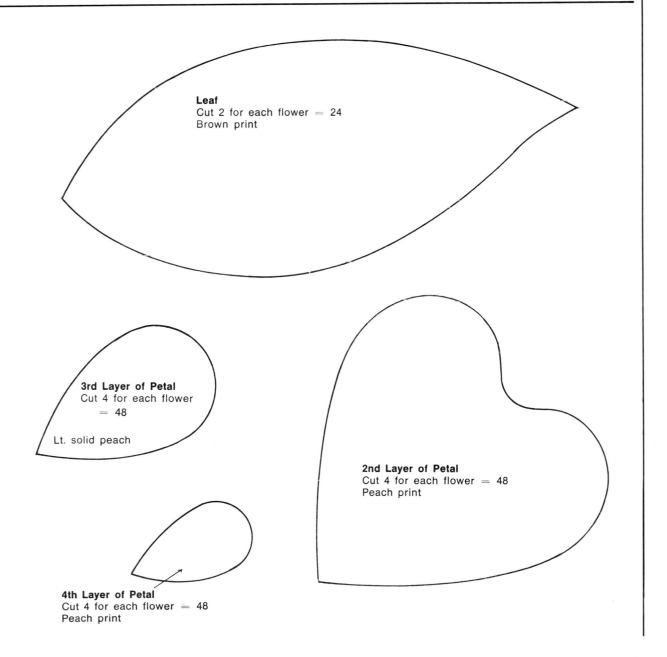

Leaf
Cut 2 for each flower = 24
Brown print

3rd Layer of Petal
Cut 4 for each flower
= 48

Lt. solid peach

2nd Layer of Petal
Cut 4 for each flower = 48
Peach print

4th Layer of Petal
Cut 4 for each flower = 48
Peach print

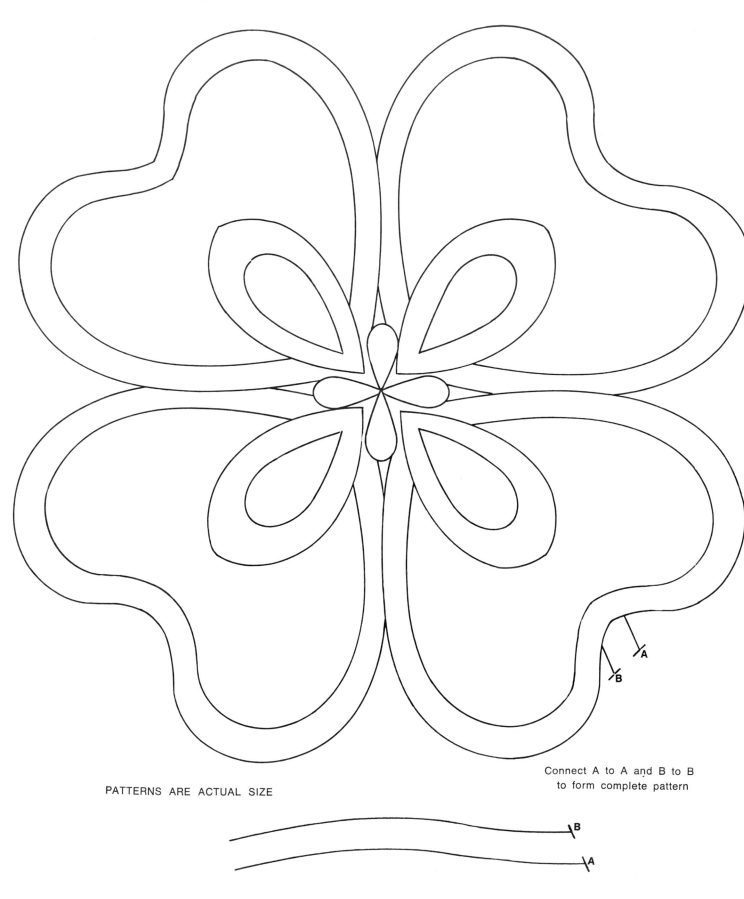

Connect A to A and B to B
to form complete pattern

PATTERNS ARE ACTUAL SIZE

EACH SQUARE EQUALS 1 INCH

Curve-Around-Two-Straight-Lines Quilting Motif

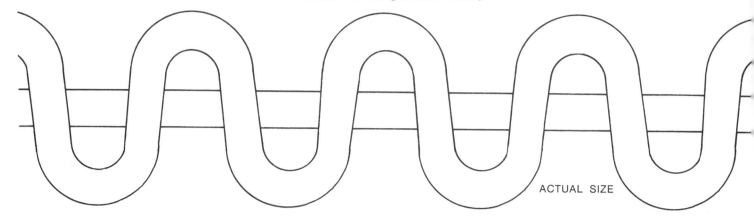

ACTUAL SIZE

Quilt Setting for Peach Blossom

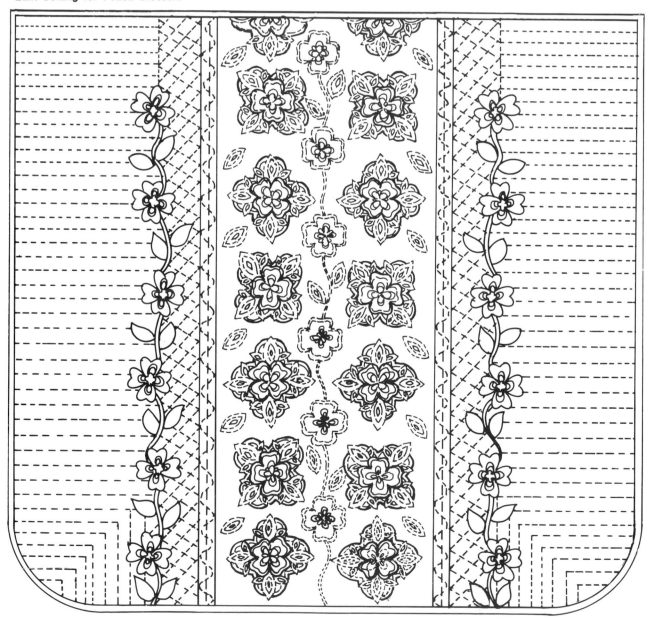

184

AMERICAN INDIAN QUILT
Shown on page 57

Materials: Cotton or cotton/polyester blend fabrics in the following colors and amounts: 7 yards cream color fabric for front and back, 2 yards brown fabric, 2 yards rust fabric, 1½ yards black fabric, 1 yard turquoise blue fabric, 1½ yards gray fabric; cream color yardage for cutting bias strips; off-white quilting thread; thin polyester quilt batt.

Quilt is approximately 64 x 82 inches finished.

This quilt is made up of a center block with an applique design and seven border rows of quilting and piecework surrounding it. See illustration of how to count the rows in this quilt.

Note: ¼-inch seam allowances are added to all cutting measurements given. On appliques, do not add seam allowances when cutting templates; draw pencil line around template onto fabric and add seam allowance when cutting. This gives you a pencil line as a guide for turning under seam allowance while appliqueing.

To make center portion of quilt cut a rectangle 42½ x 23½ from cream fabric. Piece all elements of center applique motif. Where colors appear on top of another color, applique the top piece in place on the bottom color (indicated on pattern as "applique on top of rust, applique on top of gray, etc.") after appliqueing the first layer to cream fabric. The pattern is shown on the fold so be sure to cut those pieces that fall on the fold line on the fold; those that do not fall on fold line are cut separately for each side of design, reversing for other side. The gray steps at the bottom of the design should be cut one step at a time on the fold as the brown pyramid and the rust half circle are appliqued on top of the

three steps.

Follow instuctions below to make the rows radiating out from center panel.

Row 1: From brown fabric cut two pieces 4½ x 32½ inches for top and bottom of center panel and cut two pieces 4½ x 42½ inches for sides of center panel. Using ¼-inch seams attach Row 1 to center panel.

Row 2: Piece 10 of Unit A (note that half of Unit A is shown with center pieces placed on fold; repeat for other half adding seam allowances to all measurements). Two of complete Unit A will be used for the top and bottom and three will be used for each side. Make four of Corner B, one for each corner of Row 2. Attach Row 2 to Row 1.

Row 3: From black, cut two strips 1½ x 46½ inches for top and bottom and cut two strips 1½ x 62½ inches for sides. Attach to Row 2.

Row 4: From rust, cut two strips 4½ x 54½ inches for top and bottom and cut two strips 4½ x 64½ inches for sides. Attach Row 4 to Row 3.

Row 5: This row is made by making a three-color Seminole patchwork strip according to the diagrams below:

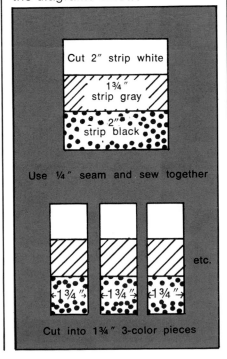

Cut 2″ strip white

1¾″ strip gray

2″ strip black

Use ¼″ seam and sew together

1¾″   1¾″   1¾″   etc.

Cut into 1¾″ 3-color pieces

Sew together again by dropping down one color. etc.

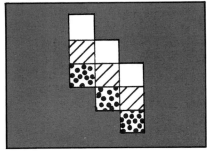

Stitch to Row 4 using as many as needed to fit each side then top and bottom. Have them meet at corners and trim off excess. You will need approximately 21 gray diamonds for top and bottom and approximately 38 gray diamonds for each side.

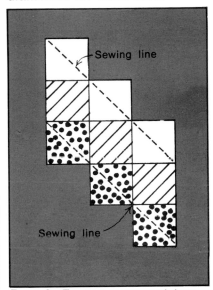

Sewing line

Sewing line

Row 6: From cream, cut two strips 1¼ x 58 inches for top and bottom and cut two strips 1¼ x 76 inches for sides. Attach to Row 5.

Row 7: This row is comprised of two piecing designs. Note that the side borders run from top of quilt to bottom, encasing ends of top and bottom borders. The first piecing design is made by sewing 2-inch wide strips of gray to 1¼-inch wide strips of blue together in long strips and then cutting them into 1¼-inch wide pieces to be used in piecing this row. These will be alternated with rust and cream pieces made the same way (rust being the 2-inch and cream being the 1¼-inch). See illustration.

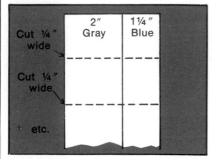

Cut ¼" wide → | 2" Gray | 1¼" Blue

Cut ¼" wide →

" etc.

You will need approximately 108 gray/blue pieces and approximately 108 rust/cream pieces to make row.
The second piecing design is a 2¾-inch square made up of four colors. See illustration.

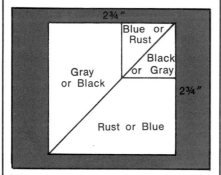

2¾"

Blue or Rust

Black or Gray

Gray or Black

2¾"

Rust or Blue

The colors change within the square and the square rotates as shown below. Note that the small square within the larger square always touches Row 6.

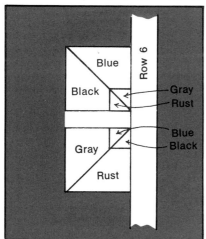

Row 6

Blue
Black → Gray
→ Rust
Gray → Blue
→ Black
Rust

There are two of these square combinations in the center of the top and bottom and two in the center of each side.
There are 1⅞ x 2¾-inch brown pieces and 1½ x 2¾-inch cream pieces separating the squares in the following sequence:

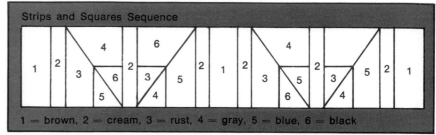

Strips and Squares Sequence

1 = brown, 2 = cream, 3 = rust, 4 = gray, 5 = blue, 6 = black

To make top of Row 7, begin in the upper left hand corner with a rust/cream piece (rust to the outside of the quilt throughout) and alternate with gray/blue (gray to the outside throughout) for twenty pieces. Attach to first brown strip of strips-and-squares sequence. Then add twenty more rust/cream and gray/blue pieces to complete top Row 7. Repeat for bottom. Sides are made the same way with 33 rust/cream and gray/blue pieces on either side of strips-and-squares sequence.
Sandwich quilt top, quilt batt and lining fabric and baste together. Quilt as following using off-white quilting thread:
Center: Quilt diagonally every two inches (forms quilted diamonds) (do not quilt over appliques). Quilt in the ditch around applique.

Row 1: Space Quilt Motif No. 1 evenly: three on top and bottom and five on each side. Use center diamond portion of motif for each corner.
Row 2: Quilt ¼ inch away from every seam line. Quilt a double line ¼ inch apart on rust portion of Unit A.
Row 3: No quilting.
Row 4: Space Quilt Motif No. 2 evenly around quilt (motif is shown as it is used at corners). Use six motifs across top and bottom and seven down each side. Quilt in the ditch along Row 3 edge.
Row 5: Quilt ¼ inch from all seam lines.
Row 6: Quilt ¼ inch from both seam lines.
Row 7: Quilt ¼ inch from all seam lines.
Cut bias binding from cream fabric and bind quilt.

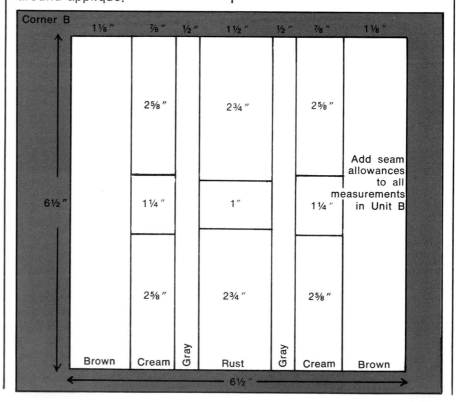

Corner B

1⅛" | ⅞" | ½" | 1½" | ½" | ⅞" | 1⅛"

2⅝" | 2¾" | 2⅝"

Add seam allowances to all measurements in Unit B

6½"

1¼" | 1" | 1¼"

2⅝" | 2¾" | 2⅝"

Brown | Cream | Gray | Rust | Gray | Cream | Brown

6½"

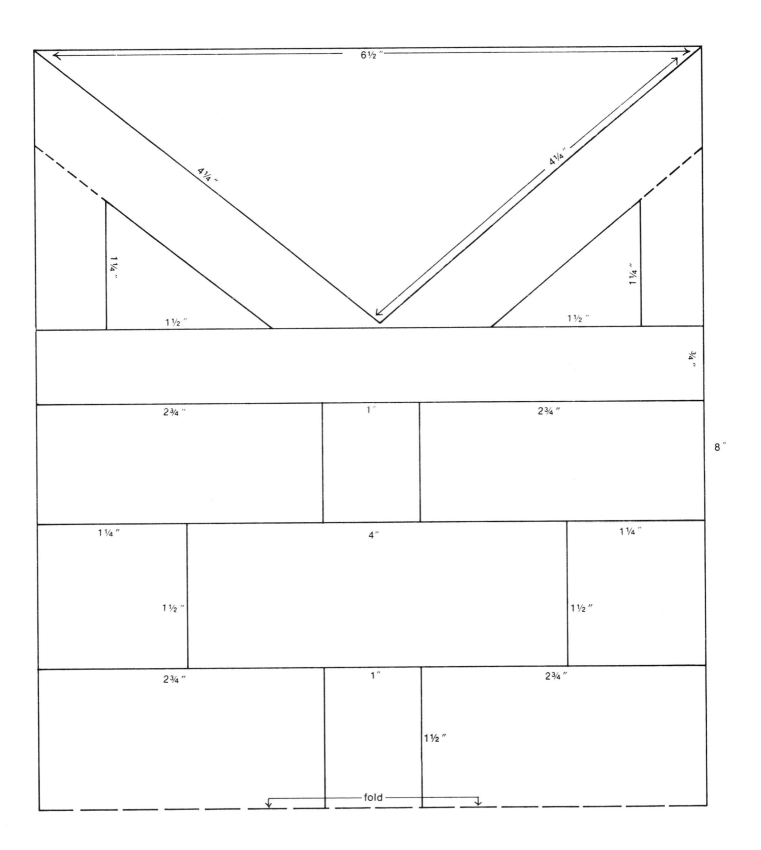

Add seam allowances to all measurements in Unit A

Quilt Motif No. 1
(Use on Row No. 1)

EACH SQUARE EQUALS 1 INCH

Quilt Motif No. 2
(Use on Row No. 4)

How to Count Rows in Quilt

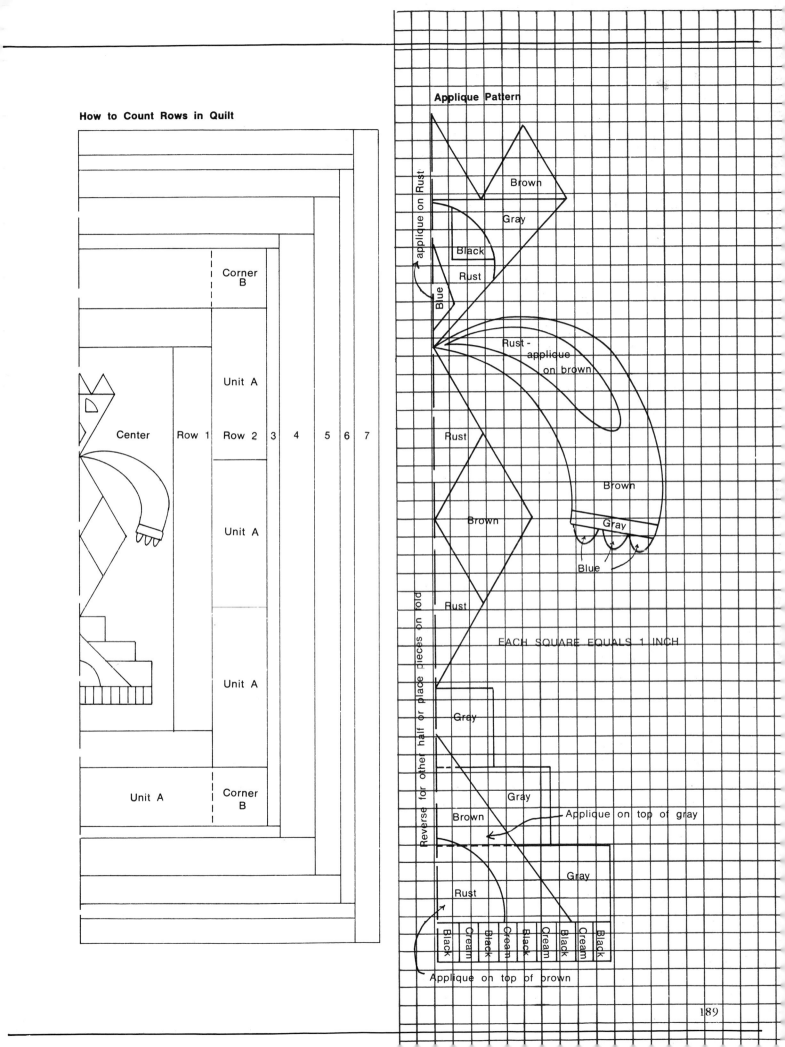

Corner B

Unit A

Center | Row 1 | Row 2 | 3 | 4 | 5 | 6 | 7

Unit A

Unit A

Unit A | Corner B

Applique Pattern

applique on Rust

Brown

Gray

Black

Rust

Blue

Rust - applique on brown

Rust

Brown

Brown

Gray

Blue

Reverse for other half or place pieces on fold

Rust

EACH SQUARE EQUALS 1 INCH

Gray

Gray

Brown

Applique on top of gray

Gray

Rust

Black | Cream | Black | Cream | Black | Cream | Black | Cream | Black

Applique on top of brown

189

Resources

One-inch grid sheets to be used for enlarging patterns are available in packages of six 25 x 38-inch sheets. The grid sheets are $3.00 plus 75¢ postage and handling from Needlecraft for Today, 4949 Byers, Ft. Worth, TX 76107.

Full-size patterns complete with instructions are available for each quilt shown in this book. Price of each pattern is as follows:

Starry Night—$2.00
Flowering Plum—$2.00
Queen's Petticoat—$2.00
Hawaiian Fruit Trees—$2.00
Stars Over Hawaii—$2.00
Christmas Star—$2.00
Sunstar—$2.00
Along the River—$2.00
Country Rose—$2.00
Jackie's Tulips—$2.00
Joanne's Quilt—$2.00
Vanishing Point—$2.00
Evolution—$2.00
Sweet Dreams—$2.00
Holy Man—$2.00
Symphony in F—$2.00
Oriental Blossom—$3.00
Peach Blossom—$2.00
American Indian—$2.00

Add 75¢ postage and handling per order (from one to nineteen patterns ordered at one time). Order from Needlecraft for Today, 4949 Byers, Ft. Worth, TX 76107.

The film, "Quilts in Women's Lives", can be ordered. It is a 28-minute, 16 mm film which sells for $450 or rents for $50. It is also available on video-cassette which sells for $400. To order write to New Day Films, P. O. Box 315, Dept. NFT, Franklin Lakes, NJ 07417. Telephone: (201) 891-8240.

A catalog of patterns for toys and dolls designed by Colette Wolff is available for $1.00 and may be obtained from Platypus, 200 W. 82nd St., Dept. QHH, New York, NY 10024.

Index

A

Applique, 65, 67-68, 73, **80-84,** 88
APPLIQUED QUILTS, 65, 73, 80-84
   Along the River, **30-31,** 60, 73, **138-144**
   American Indian, **56-57,** 84-85, **185-189**
   Christmas Star, **26-27,** 59, 65, 67, 73, 81, 85, 92, **127-132**
   Country Rose, **32-33,** 60, 63-65, 68, 73, **145-147**
   Flowering Plum, **18-19,** 59-60, 62, 65, 80, 85, 93, 97, **111-120**
   Hawaiian Fruit Trees, **22-23,** 62, 65, 84, 88, **121-123**
   Jackie's Tulips, **34-35,** 62, 85, 92, **148-153**
   Oriental Blossom, **52-53,** 60, 62, 65, **173-179**
   Peach Blossom, **54-55,** 59, 65, 84-85, 93, 97, **180-184**
   Stars Over Hawaii, **24-25,** 62, 68, 73, 81, 84-85, **124-126**
   Sunstar, **28-29,** 60, 84, **133-137**
Along the River Quilt, **30-31,** 60, 73, **138-144**
American Indian Quilt, **56-57,** 84-85, **185-189**
Assembling the Top, 84-85

B

Binding the Edge, 90, **93-97**
BOOKS, 21
   Anyone Can Quilt, 21
   Art of Embroidery, 21
   New Discoveries in American Quilts, 21
   Portrait of America, 21
   Quilts in America, 21
   Twentieth Century Folk Art & Artists, 21
Borkowski, Mary, 7, 8-9, **21,** 22, 24, 26, 28, 30, 32, 34, 59-60, 63-64, 67, 82-83, 91-92

C

Christmas Star Quilt, **26-27,** 59, 65, 67, 73, 81, 85, 92, **127-132**
Color, **59-64,** 65-67, 78, 80, 82, 85, 88, 90, 92
Color Schemes, **60,** 61-64, 66
Country Rose Quilt, **32-33,** 60, 63-65, 68, 73, **145-147**
Cutting, 70-73

D

Decisions in the Fabric Store, 66-67
DESIGNERS,
   Borkowski, Mary, 7, 8-9, **21,** 22, 24, 26, 28, 30, 32, 34, 59-60, 63-64, 67, 82-83, 91-92
   Guillow, Kathy Sue, 7, 8-9, **51,** 52, 54, 56, 59, 60
   Logan, Diann, 7, 8-9, **37,** 38, 40, 42, 44, 46, 48, 59-60, 63, 65
   Wolff, Colette, 7, 8, **13,** 14, 16, 18, 59
Display and Care, 97

E

Enlarging, 66, **68**
Evolution Quilt, **42-43,** 65, 73, **159-162**

F

Flowering Plum Quilt, **18-19,** 59-60, 62, 65, 80, 85, 93, 97, **111-120**

G

Guillow, Kathy Sue, 7, 8-9, **51,** 52, 54, 56, 59, 60

H

Hawaiian Fruit Trees Quilt, **22-23,** 62, 65, 84, 88, **121-123**
Holy Man Quilt, **46-47,** 65, **166-169**

I

INSTRUCTIONS, 99-189
   Along the River, 138-144
   American Indian, 185-189
   Christmas Star, 127-132
   Country Rose, 145-147
   Evolution, 159-162
   Flowering Plum, 111-120
   Hawaiian Fruit Trees, 121-123
   Holy Man, 166-169
   Jackie's Tulips, 148-153
   Joanne's Quilt, 154-155
   Oriental Blossom, 173-179
   Peach Blossom, 180-184
   Queen's Petticoat, 105-110
   Starry Night, 99-104
   Stars Over Hawaii, 124-126
   Sunstar, 133-137
   Sweet Dreams, 163-165
   Symphony in F, 170-172
   Vanishing Point, 156-158

J

Jackie's Tulips, **34-35,** 62, 85, 92, **148-153**
Joanne's Quilt, **38-39,** 62-65, **154-155**

L

Logan, Diann, 7, 8-9, **37,** 38, 40, 42, 44, 46, 48, 59-60, 63, 65

O

Oriental Blossom Quilt, **52-53,** 60, 62, 65, **173-179**

P

PATTERNS, 87, **99-189**
   Along the River, 138-144
   American Indian, 185-189
   Christmas Star, 127-132
   Country Rose, 145-147
   Evolution, 159-162
   Flowering Plum, 111-120
   Hawaiian Fruit Trees, 121-123
   Holy Man, 166-169
   Jackie's Tulips, 148-153
   Joanne's Quilt, 154-155
   Oriental Blossom, 173-179
   Peach Blossom, 180-184
   Queen's Petticoat, 105-110
   Starry Night, 99-104
   Stars Over Hawaii, 124-126
   Sunstar, 133-137
   Sweet Dreams, 163-165
   Symphony in F, 170-172
   Vanishing Point, 156-158
Peach Blossom Quilt, **54-55,** 59, 65, 84-85, 93, 97, **180-184**
PIECED QUILTS, 65, 68
   American Indian, **56-57,** 84-85, **185-189**
   Evolution, **42-43,** 65, 73, **159-162**
   Holy Man, **46-47,** 65, **166-169**
   Joanne's Quilt, **38-39,** 62-65, **154-155**
   Queen's Petticoat, **16-17,** 62, 65, 84-85, **105-110**
   Starry Night, 13, **14-15,** 60, 62, 65-66, 72-74, 84, **99-104**

Sunstar, **28-29,** 60, 84, **133-137**
Sweet Dreams, **44-45,** 59, 62, 65, 84, **163-165**
Symphony in F, **48-49, 170-172**
Vanishing Point, **40-41,** 60, 62, 65, 74, 84, 88, **156-158**
Piecing, 68, **73-80,** 84, 88

Q

Queen's Petticoat Quilt, **16-17,** 62, 65, 84-85, **105-110**
Quilting, 65, 69, **85-88, 88-93**
QUILTS,
Along the River, **30-31,** 60, 73, **138-144**
American Indian, **56-57,** 84-85, **185-189**
Christmas Star, **26-27,** 59, 65, 67, 73, 81, 85, 92, **127-132**
Country Rose, **32-33,** 60, 63-65, 68, 73, **145-147**
Evolution, **42-43,** 65, 73, **159-162**
Flowering Plum, **18-19,** 59-60, 62, 65, 80, 85, 93, 97, **111-120**
Hawaiian Fruit Trees, **22-23,** 62, 65, 84, 88, **121-123**
Holy Man, **46-47,** 65, **166-169**
Jackie's Tulips, **34-35,** 62, 85, 92, **148-153**
Joanne's Quilt, **38-39,** 62-65, **154-155**
Oriental Blossom, **52-53,** 60, 62, 65, **173-179**
Peach Blossom, **54-55,** 59, 65, 84-85, 93, 97, **180-184**
Queen's Petticoat, **16-17,** 62, 65, 84-85, **105-110**
Starry Night, 13, **14-15,** 60, 62, 65-66, 72-74, 84, **99-104**
Stars Over Hawaii, **24-25,** 62, 68, 73, 81, 84-85, **124-126**
Sunstar, **28-29,** 60, 84, **133-137**
Sweet Dreams, **44-45,** 59, 62, 65, 84, **163-165**
Symphony in F, **48-49, 170-172**
Vanishing Point, **40-41,** 60, 62, 65, 74, 84, 88, **156-158**

R

RESOURCES, 190

S

Starry Night Quilt, 13, **14-15,** 60, 62, 65-66, 72-74, 84, **99-104**

Stars Over Hawaii Quilt, **24-25,** 62, 68, 73, 81, 84-85, **124-126**
Sunstar Quilt, **28-29,** 60, 84, **133-137**
Sweet Dreams Quilt, **44-45,** 59, 62, 65, 84, **163-165**
Symphony in F Quilt, **48-49, 170-172**

T

TECHNIQUES, 59-97
Applique, 80-84
Assembling the Top, 84-85
Binding the Edge, 93-97
Cutting, 70-73
Decisions in the Fabric Store, 66-67
Display and Care, 97
Enlarging Chore, That, 68
Help for Color Shy Quilters, 59-64
Nuts and Bolts, The, 67
Piecing the Blocks, 73-80
Quilting: The Design, 85-88
Quilting: The Process, 88-93
Sensibly Speaking, 65
Signature, The, 97
Size Question, The, **65-66,** 68
Templates, 68-69
Templates, **68-69,** 70, 72-73, 80, 83, 87

V

Vanishing Point Quilt, **40-41,** 60, 62, 65, 74, 84, 88, **156-158**

W

Wolff, Colette, 7, 8, **13,** 14, 16, 18, 59